Drug Therapy and Personality Disorders

Psychiatric Disorders
Drugs and Psychology for the Mind and Body

Psychiatric Disorders: Drugs and Psychology for the Mind and Body

Drug Therapy and Personality Disorders

BY SHIRLEY BRINKERHOFF

MASON CREST PUBLISHERS
PHILADELPHIA

Mason Crest Publishers Inc.
370 Reed Road
Broomall, Pennsylvania 19008
(866) MCP-BOOK (toll free)

First printing
1 2 3 4 5 6 7 8 9 10
Brinkerhoff, Shirley.
Drug therapy and personality disorders / by Shirley Brinkerhoff.
p. cm.—(Psychiatric disorders: drugs and psychology for the mind and body)
Summary: Describes the characteristics and drug treatment of personality disorders, as well as alternative therapies. Includes bibliographical references and index.
1. Personality disorders—Juvenile literature. 2. Personality disorders—Chemotherapy—Juvenile literature. 3. Personality disorders—Treatment—Juvenile literature. [1. Personality disorders. 2. Mental illness.] I. Title. II. Series.
RC554.B75 2004
616.85'8—dc21
2003004404

ISBN 1-59084-571-4
ISBN 1-59084-559-5 (series)

Design by Lori Holland.
Composition by Bytheway Publishing Services, Binghamton, New York.
Cover design by Benjamin Stewart.
Printed and bound in the Hashemite Kingdom of Jordan.

This book is meant to educate and should not be used as an alternative to appropriate medical care. Its creators have made every effort to ensure that the information presented is accurate— but it is not intended to substitute for the help and services of trained professionals.

Picture Credits:
Artville: pp. 25, 26, 28, 35, 39, 47, 50, 64, 80, 98, 100, 110. Autumn Libal: pp. 52, 53, 66. Benjamin Stewart: pp. 18, 71. Digivision: pp. 81, 82, 115, 118. National Library of Medicine (WHO): p. 120. PhotoDisc: pp. 10, 23, 30, 72, 74, 76, 85, 88, 102, 105, 106, 112, 116. Quigmans: pp. 32, 33, 40, 79, 94. Rubberball: p. 20. Stockbyte: pp. 12, 14, 93. The individuals in these images are models, and the images are for illustrative purposes only.

CONTENTS

INTRODUCTION

by Mary Ann Johnson

Teenagers have reason to be interested in psychiatric disorders and their treatment. Friends, family members, and even teens themselves may experience one of these disorders. Using scenarios adolescents will understand, this series explains various psychiatric disorders and the drugs that treat them.

Diagnosis and treatment of psychiatric disorders in children between six and eighteen years old are well studied and documented in the scientific journals. In 1998, Roberts and colleagues identified and reviewed fifty-two research studies that attempted to identify the overall prevalence of child and adolescent psychiatric disorders. Estimates of prevalence in this review ranged from one percent to nearly 51 percent. Various other studies have reported similar findings. Needless to say, many children and adolescents are suffering from psychiatric disorders and are in need of treatment.

Many children have more than one psychiatric disorder, which complicates their diagnoses and treatment plans. Psychiatric disorders often occur together. For instance, a person with a sleep disorder may also be depressed; a teenager with attention-deficit/hyperactivity disorder (ADHD) may also have a substance-use disorder. In psychiatry, we call this comorbidity. Much research addressing this issue has led to improved diagnosis and treatment.

The most common child and adolescent psychiatric disorders are anxiety disorders, depressive disorders, and ADHD. Sleep disorders, sexual disorders, eating disorders, substance-abuse disorders, and psychotic disorders are also quite common. This series has volumes that address each of these disorders.

Major depressive disorders have been the most commonly diagnosed mood disorders for children and adolescents. Researchers don't agree as to how common mania and bipolar disorder are in children. Some experts believe that manic episodes in children and adolescents are underdiagnosed. Many times, a mood disturbance may co-occur with another psychiatric disorder. For instance, children with ADHD may also be depressed. ADHD is just one psychiatric disorder that is a major health concern for children, adolescents, and adults. Studies of ADHD have reported prevalence rates among children that range from two to 12 percent.

Failure to understand or seek treatment for psychiatric disorders puts children and young adults at risk of developing substance-use disorders. For example, recent research indicates that those with ADHD who were treated with medication were 85 percent less likely to develop a substance-use disorder. Results like these emphasize the importance of timely diagnosis and treatment.

Early diagnosis and treatment may prevent these children from developing further psychological problems. Books like those in this series provide important information, a vital first step toward increased awareness of psychological disorders; knowledge and understanding can shed light on even the most difficult subject. These books should never, however, be viewed as a substitute for professional consultation. Psychiatric testing and an evaluation by a licensed professional are recommended to determine the needs of the child or adolescent and to establish an appropriate treatment plan.

FOREWORD

by Donald Esherick

We live in a society filled with technology—from computers surfing the Internet to automobiles operating on gas and batteries. In the midst of this advanced society, diseases, illnesses, and medical conditions are treated and often cured with the administration of drugs, many of which were unknown thirty years ago. In the United States, we are fortunate to have an agency, the Food and Drug Administration (FDA), which monitors the development of new drugs and then determines whether the new drugs are safe and effective for use in human beings.

When a new drug is developed, a pharmaceutical company usually intends that drug to treat a single disease or family of diseases. The FDA reviews the company's research to determine if the drug is safe for use in the population at large and if it effectively treats the targeted illnesses. When the FDA finds that the drug is safe and effective, it approves the drug for treating that specific disease or condition. This is called the labeled indication.

During the routine use of the drug, the pharmaceutical company and physicians often observe that a drug treats other medical conditions besides what is indicated in the labeling. While the labeling will not include the treatment of the particular condition, a physician can still prescribe the drug to a patient with this disease. This is known as an unlabeled or off-label indication. This series contains information about both the labeled and off-label indications of psychiatric drugs.

I have reviewed the books in this series from the perspective of the pharmaceutical industry and the FDA, specifically focusing on the labeled indications, uses, and known side effects of these drugs. Further information can be found on the FDA's Web page (www.FDA.gov).

Each person's personality consists of many factors.

1 | Defining the Disorder

What makes people who they are?

Consider Lynette Corby. When she fills out a questionnaire for her on-line dating service, she writes that she has blue eyes, blonde hair, and stands five feet ten and a half inches tall. She also adds that she's a Canadian, a Caucasian, and works on a road crew, helping direct oncoming cars.

Lynette receives nine e-mails from men who are interested in the possibility of dating a tall, blue-eyed blonde. But e-mail number ten, from a man named Rick, is different from the other responses Lynette receives. It reads:

> I need to know more about who you really *are,* Lynette.
> Tell me how you act on Christmas morning when you get

the present you've been dreaming of. Tell me how you respond when you're all dressed up and a speeding car splashes mud on your clothes, or when you don't get the raise you hoped for at work. How do you react to telemarketers who call, or to family members who try to borrow money? Do you plan to work for a road crew all your life? Or do you have secret aspirations to do something else, like write novels or be a prison guard?

What Rick is really saying in his e-mail is that he wants to know about Lynette's *personality*—her characteristic patterns of behavior and thought in many different circumstances.

Human beings are alike in many ways. There are broad similarities in behavior and thought patterns, so much so that we can categorize people into personality types (an example is what we call Type A personality—competitive, ag-

A "Type A personality" is competitive and aggressive.

gressive, achievement oriented). In spite of these similarities, however, personality is really a study of the differences in how individual people think and behave.

PERSONALITY THEORY

Theories of personality abound. Some authorities on this subject say that personality is the result of *physiological*, or *innate* factors. Others attribute personality to the interactions between innate factors and an individual's experiences. Personality is a very complicated phenomenon, as evidenced by the fact that there have been so many theories about it throughout history.

As far back as the time of the ancient Greeks, the physician Hippocrates taught that differences in people's behavior occurred because they had a predominance of one type of "humor," the word he used for body fluid. For instance, people who were calm or passive had one dominant humor, while those who were impulsive or temperamental had another.

Around 1900, contemporary personality theory began with the teachings of Sigmund Freud, the Austrian physician who founded psychoanalysis. Freud taught that personality arises from social interactions, which begin in the mother–child relationship, and that a personality is formed during the first few years of life. Psychoanalysis puts great emphasis on the unconscious processes that influence human behavior. According to Bruce Bower, however, in a 1999 issue of *Science News*, "researchers began to turn away from this Freud-inspired perspective by mid-century."

Other personality theories followed, including Gordon Allport's trait theory, which emphasizes an individual's traits, or tendencies to behave in a consistent manner over

time in various situations; situationism, which emphasizes the situation above the trait; and interactionism, which takes into account the importance of both trait and situation.

Physiological theories hold that the physical differences in people determine or influence their type of personality. Ernst Kretschmer, a German psychiatrist, believed personality was the result of a person's body build. For instance, he thought that short people are more likely to be social, friendly, and lively.

Psychiatrist W. H. Sheldon thought that people had different personalities related to their body type. The three body types he mentioned were:

- endomorphs—those with heavy, rounded bodies
- mesomorphs—those with muscular, athletic bodies
- ectomorphs—those with thin, angular bodies

According to Sheldon, an endomorph has a heavy, rounded body—and a particular set of personality characteristics. Researchers today see no evidence to support Sheldon's theory.

Diagnostic and Statistical Manual

There are thousands of mental health care professionals around the world who treat patients for a wide variety of disorders. Added to their number are the thousands of research scientists who study mental disorders, their causes, and their treatment. Agreement among these individuals as to diagnosing different disorders can be extremely difficult.

The *Diagnostic and Statistical Manual* (DSM) was developed to address this problem. It was written to make diagnoses more reliable (that is, to increase agreement among people making diagnoses) and to place more emphasis on the person's behavior and feelings, rather than assuming knowledge of some underlying cause of the condition.

In order to produce an accurate diagnosis, the DSM takes into account five factors (called axes) to classify the individual being diagnosed:

1. primary diagnosis
2. typical personality characteristics
3. relevant physical disorders
4. past stress the individual has been exposed to
5. how the person has coped with past stress

Research has not proved that Sheldon's idea was correct, nor has science backed up many other past personality theories. Today, psychologists look at things a bit differently.

WHAT ARE PERSONALITY DISORDERS?

The subject of personality is complex, and the related subject of personality disorders is also one of considerable complexity, so much so that it frequently undergoes revision.

By the 1980s, the American Psychiatric Association rejected many of the earlier approaches to defining personality and allowed their official diagnostic manual of mental diseases to undergo an extensive revision. For the first time the manual included separate diagnoses of personality disorders. The diagnoses rely on sets of specific, clinically observed symptoms. The most recent edition of the *Diagnostic and Statistical Manual of Mental Disorders* (the DSM-IV) describes ten personality disorders and mentions two others worthy of further study.

A personality disorder is currently defined in the DSM-IV as "an enduring pattern of inner experience and behavior that deviates markedly from the expectations of the individual's culture, is pervasive and inflexible, has an onset in adolescence or early adulthood, is stable over time, and leads to distress or impairment."

Although each personality disorder has differing symptoms specific to that disorder (for more on individual disorders, see chapter two), most people with a personality disorder have these general features:

- The individual's responses to stress are inflexible and maladaptive.
- The individual has difficulty relating to others, which impairs both work and social relationships.
- The individual lacks insight into her condition. Rather than seeing her symptomatic behavior as a problem that needs to be corrected, the individual with a personality disorder expresses her belief that "this is just the way I am."

Although many people feel that the DSM-IV has been a great step forward in defining the personality disorders, there is already disagreement about how the disorders are dealt with in this latest version of the manual. For instance, some practitioners ask how they are to define "an enduring pattern of inner experience," one phrase from the manual. Some have gone so far as to suggest yet another revision. The definitions of personality disorders are "ripe for an overhaul," according to psychiatrist John G. Gunderson of McLean Hospital in Belmont, Massachusetts.

Jack M. Gorman, M.D., writes in *The New Psychiatry*:

> Diagnosis is key; treatments are specifically linked to the exact disorder the patient suffers from. . . . But we have a terrible time defining what *neurotic* actually is. . . . The DSM system has attempted to supply us with categories of neurotic illnesses, called *personality disorders*. . . . But many people feel these categories do not sufficiently capture all the nuances of human character and therefore do not help us when we think there is something abnormal about someone's personality.

In spite of the difficulties in defining personality disorders, there is enough agreement on them that an explanation of each can be given. The DSM-IV groups the ten recognized personality disorders into three clusters:

CLUSTER	DISORDER	PATIENT'S BEHAVIOR
Cluster A	paranoid schizoid schizotypal	appears odd or eccentric
Cluster B	antisocial borderline histrionic narcissistic	appears overly emotional, unstable, self-dramatizing
Cluster C	avoidant dependent obsessive-compulsive	appears tense, anxiety-ridden

GLOSSARY

pervasive: Tends to spread throughout.

inflexible: Stubborn, unyielding, unshakeable.

deviate: To turn aside from a standard.

WHAT IS THE DIFFERENCE BETWEEN A NEGATIVE TRAIT AND A DISORDER?

People are sometimes disturbed by reading definitions of the personality disorders, because the majority of us experience at least some of these traits or behavior patterns at one time or another. The issue is one of degree and time, however. The DSM-IV definition highlights the qualities of true personality disorders in the following quoted words or phrases: they involve "enduring" patterns, ones that are "*pervasive* and *inflexible*," that are "stable over time," that "*deviate* markedly from the expectations of the individual's culture," and lead to a person's "distress or impairment."

If, during a distressing time in a person's life, he acts in some of the ways described in the personality disorder defi-

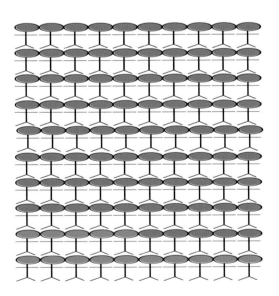

About fifteen out of every one hundred North Americans suffer from a personality disorder.

nitions, his actions could be only a temporary problem, the kind most people face at one time or another. Many of these people eventually return to "normal behavior," the type of behavior their culture expects, indicating that the behavior was not a true personality disorder.

However, when traits are so prominent and rigid that they cause dysfunction in a person's life, and when this situation is one of long standing, then a disorder may indeed be present.

In addition to the qualities mentioned above, individuals with personality disorders often view their symptoms as consistent with their own self-image, or ego-syntonic, and not as problems that need treatment. This means that very few people with personality disorders seek treatment on their own for their conditions.

HOW PREVALENT ARE PERSONALITY DISORDERS?

An accurate number of how many people have personality disorders is difficult to determine. Some of the personality disorders—such as **borderline** and **antisocial** disorders—by their very nature attract more attention than others. A young man with antisocial disorder, for example, is far more likely to get into trouble with the law and, as a result, have his disorder noted and diagnosed than is a young man who has avoidant personality disorder and shies away from any situation or relationship where he might face rejection. The latter person might live out his life without ever being diagnosed or receiving help.

Even so, the best estimate is that about 15 percent of North Americans suffer from a personality disorder. In some cases, individuals have more than one disorder.

GLOSSARY

borderline: A personality disorder characterized by unstable interpersonal relationships, self-image, emotions; and impulse control.

antisocial: A personality disorder characterized by superficiality, lack of empathy or remorse, inability to feel guilt, poor impulse control, and unconcern for societal norms. Previously referred to as psychopathic personality.

A personality disorder may have its roots in a child's earliest interactions with her family.

Judging Others

One difficulty in understanding personality comes from our own perception of other people and our natural instinct to trust our first impressions about them rather than really get to know them. In 1979, *Psychology Today* reported on a special version of *What's My Line?* played at the annual conference of the Institute of Personnel Managers in England, as a test of intuitive powers. Nearly three hundred participants, many of whom were personnel managers, were shown short videotapes of nine men and a woman discussing several different topics. The managers were then asked to rate the people they observed in several different categories.

The participants were often not accurate. The test showed that the participants tended to like the people they perceived to be like themselves and tended to consider them to be more intelligent. According to Freedman, author of *Introductory Pschology*, the participants showed a preference for the people they thought were intelligent, but their accuracy in assessing IQ on the basis of intuition was on average 22 (on a scale that ranged from zero being pure chance to 100 percent accuracy). The participants who were not involved in personnel work actually scored better than those who were, and men scored a little higher than women.

HOW DO PERSONALITY DISORDERS ARISE?

Due to the broad spectrum of disorders in this category, no single cause for all the disorders can be named. However, most mental health care professionals agree that in the case of some of the personality disorders, the origin may be in the interaction between a child's individual temperament and her family environment. Because developmental factors contribute significantly to personality disorders, some mental health professionals actually call personality disorders "developmental damage."

Psychosocial Causes

The interactions between a child and her family that contribute to the development of personality disorders may be extremely negative, involving situations such as child abuse. In a study of more than 900 U.S. military personnel, 57 percent of patients who had a history of childhood physical and sexual abuse developed personality disorders. Patients with antisocial personality disorder are likely to have experienced severe physical punishment or abusive treatment from their parents during childhood.

According to several research studies, adults who have borderline personality disorder are likely to have been victimized by physical and sexual abuse during childhood. One study of both male and female patients with borderline personality disorder found that 71 percent had been sexually abused, 42 percent had been physically abused, and 65 percent had a history of multiple abuses.

Other situations in which interactions between a child and his family contribute to the development of personality disorders may involve situations that do not appear on the surface to be as extreme as child abuse, but are still very negative. Gorman, in *The New Psychiatry*, gives an example concerning a child who experiences neglect or emotional deprivation. He suggests that such a child, lacking the admiration and love all children need from their parents, might build a fantasy world with himself at the center, loved by everyone. This pattern may then become the foundation for developing a narcissistic personality disorder. "I do believe . . . that neglectful and inconsistent parents are fully capable of producing narcissistic personality disorder," writes Gorman.

Rebecca J. Frey in *Personality Disorders* writes a scenario about an active child with very nervous or high-strung parents who are constantly trying to restrain him. Such

A child or adolescent who feels victimized is more likely to have a personality disorder as an adult.

parents may be displeased with an active child, and the child may eventually develop avoidant personality disorder in response to his parent's disapproval and evident frustration.

In some cases, parents may not even be around to notice their child's needs, a situation that can contribute to other disorders, such as antisocial personality disorder. Parental absence may have many causes, from being deployed as a soldier in a war, to divorce, or incarceration. In the absence of a parent or other caring, involved adult, a child cannot internalize his parent's values, a necessary factor in the development of morality. In *Introductory Psychology*, Freedman writes:

> in homes where no adult takes an interest in or expresses love to a child, the conscience does not develop and the individual fails to be socialized in this very critical way. It seems likely that this is at least one possible cause of antisocial personality. Another possibility is that highly inconsistent discipline and attention, even from the same person, prevents the child from forming normal values.

This form of child rearing allows the child to grow up without a clear understanding of what is right and what is wrong. Behaviorists believe that individuals learn their behavior by testing behaviors to see which is successful. Studies have shown that people with antisocial personality disorder frequently have fathers with the same disorder, and the child often observes and mimics the father's behavior.

In some cases, patients who will later develop personality disorders grow up in homes that do not appear to have more than the normal daily stresses we all experience. Medical researchers ask why some people develop disorders under these circumstances, while others grow up relatively unharmed by the stress.

Some kinds of child rearing practices may place the child in an emotional prison.

Aspects of our personalities are determined by our genetic heritage from our parents.

This discussion brings up a debate that has gone on for years among health care professionals—the nature versus nurture debate. In this case, nature stands for the influence of a person's inherited traits on personality development. Nurture stands for a person's environment, including family members, living conditions, and socioeconomic status. The debate is over how much of our behavior is inborn and how much is learned. In other words, does nature or nurture play the more important role in determining personality development?

Studies show that both genetic makeup and environment play a part in forming personality. Heredity can *predispose* an individual to behave in a certain way, and environment can reinforce that predisposition. Mental health professionals suspect that heredity plays some part in contributing to *paranoid*, *schizotypal*, antisocial, and borderline personality disorders. These factors are not yet completely understood, but researchers continue to study and debate the issue in hope of gaining a clearer understanding of the process of personality development, as well as the development of personality disorders.

Neurophysiological Factors

Some studies suggest associations between central nervous system activity and personality disorders. According to some researchers, schizotypal and borderline personality disorders have been associated with increased activity in the *dopamine* and norepinephrine systems. These researchers point out that decreased serotonin activity may play a role in the impulsive, aggressive behavior of those with antisocial personality disorders. Many researchers believe that low levels of serotonin may be an inherited deficiency and might trigger the impulsive violence and aggression that are the trademarks of antisocial personality disorder.

GLOSSARY

predispose: To make receptive, beforehand.

paranoid: A personality disorder characterized by pervasive mistrust and suspiciousness.

schizotypal: A personality disorder characterized by thought disturbances, eccentric behaviors, and a difficulty in maintaining close relationships.

dopamine: A neurotransmitter found in the brain that has an effect on some psychoses and movement.

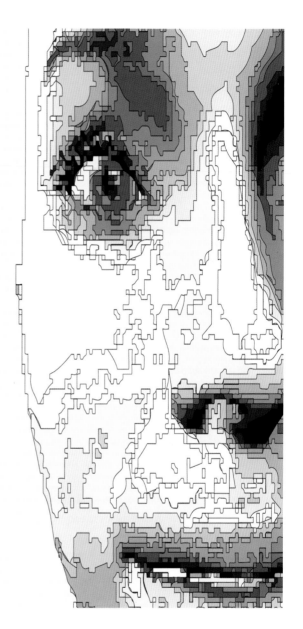

Personality is a complicated mosaic of factors.

THE PERSONALITY DISORDERS DEALT WITH IN THIS BOOK

Because the scope of this series focuses on psychiatric drugs and the mental disorders they treat, only the personality disorders that can be treated with psychiatric drugs (though drugs are not used in every case) will be included. These disorders include: paranoid, schizoid, schizotypal, borderline, obsessive-compulsive, and, in some cases, avoidant. In the next chapter, these disorders will be dealt with in more detail.

Medical doctors, psychiatrists, and advanced practice nurses are all qualified to treat and diagnose personality disorders.

2 | Personality Disorders That May Be Treated with Psychiatric Drugs

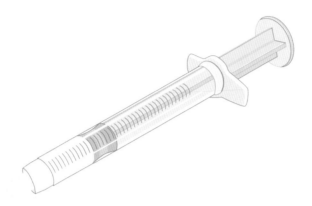

Professional mental health care workers do not always agree completely on when psychiatric drugs should and should not be used in treating personality disorders. Often, the drugs prescribed are used to treat a disorder that co-exists with the personality disorder, such as depression or behavioral problems. In some cases, treatment of these *co-existing* disorders is necessary for therapy and other treatments of the personality disorder to be more effective.

CLUSTER A PERSONALITY DISORDERS

Paranoid, schizoid, and schizotypal personality disorders are grouped together in the DSM-IV as Cluster A. While these diseases are not actual *schizophrenia*, they are sub-types of the disease, and they include many schizophrenic behaviors. However, the behaviors of those with Cluster A personality disorders are much less severe than the symptoms experienced by individuals with schizophrenia. People with paranoid, schizoid, and schizotypal personalities may experience ***psychotic episodes***, but these episodes are typically brief.

Individuals with one of the Cluster A personality disorders can appear to others to be odd or eccentric and can often seem emotionally withdrawn. When in the presence of other people, they may display unusual ideas or speech patterns, or they may be extremely anxious or detached.

The patients of traditional psychotherapists lie on a couch and analyze their pasts. . .

. . .but many modern psychiatrists rely more on medication than talk.

Paranoid Personality Disorder

Carl always expected trouble from his coworkers, particularly when he started a new job. And starting a new job was a frequent experience for Carl, because he'd lost several jobs in the past decade.

An intelligent man, Carl had completed a course in electronics at a local technical college and had never had trouble finding a job. In fact, each time he was hired, his supervisor expected great things from him based on Carl's excellent grades on his college transcripts and on the experience he listed.

Within a week or two of beginning each job, however, trouble always began, usually when Carl accused a coworker of "having it in for me," or "trying to make me look bad." The coworker, often caught off guard by such accusations, would sometimes react in fury. That often began an

interpersonal problem between the two workers, a problem that usually escalated into outright antagonism.

As Carl became more and more convinced that his coworker was "out to get him," he became increasingly suspicious and watchful of everyone around him, which made it hard for him to get his work done. Inevitably, arguments erupted, and although Carl prided himself on his objectivity and rationality, once he was convinced he had an enemy at work, he stubbornly refused to cooperate with that person. Instead, he spent his time trying to prove that his suspicions were correct.

When another worker received a raise or a promotion, Carl experienced intense jealousy, convinced that the situation only proved his suspicions—that he had, in some way, been undermined. When anyone tried to point out to Carl that much of his trouble was because of his suspicious, negative view of other people, he refused to discuss it. "This is the way I see things," he said.

According to the DSM-IV, the following are some typical features of paranoid personality disorder:

- a pattern of distrust and suspicion of other people
- assuming that other people will harm, deceive, or exploit them
- preoccupation with doubts about their friends' or associates' trustworthiness or loyalty
- reluctance to confide in others, for fear the information divulged will be used against them
- reading negative hidden messages into things people say and do
- readiness to perceive insults or injuries; bearing grudges
- suspicion of spouse or sexual partner's fidelity

A person with paranoid personality disorder may feel as though everyone is looking at him or talking about him behind his back.

Schizoid Personality Disorder

When Allan graduated from college and took a third-shift job monitoring the surveillance cameras at a local weapons factory, his parents began to hope he would finally show some interest in dating.

"Now that he's finished his degree . . ." his mother said.

"And gotten a good job . . ." his father added.

"Maybe now he'll start thinking about finding a wife. You know, maybe even starting a family," his mother finished.

Allan's parents smiled at each other, hoping that now, perhaps, things would be different for their son. But all through Allan's twenties, and on into his thirties, his schedule remained the same: Work all night. Go home and sleep till mid-afternoon. Make dinner and play computer games or watch TV until time for work.

By the time Allan entered his forties, his parents were finally beginning to understand. Allan had no intention of changing. It wasn't that he was shy. It wasn't that he hadn't met the right woman yet (although his parents had often tried to remedy that). He simply had no interest in other people or in their lives.

According to the DSM-IV, the following are two typical features of schizoid personality disorder: a long-standing pattern of social indifference and detachment and restricted emotional reactions. These two traits often manifest themselves as:

- neither desiring nor enjoying close relationships (with family or otherwise)
- preferring solitary activities
- little or no interest in sexual experiences with others
- little or no pleasure in activities
- no close friends beyond immediate family members
- indifference to praise or criticism
- displaying coldness and detachment

Schizotypal Personality Disorder

MaryAnn was always considered the "odd" one in high school. While the other girls in her class spent hours shopping for carefully matched, name-brand outfits at the outlet mall, MaryAnn pulled on whatever clothing her mother brought home for her with barely a glance at it.

"Don't you care how you *look?*" her mother pleaded when MaryAnn wore the same shirt to school three days in a row.

MaryAnn shook her head, unconcerned.

"If ever a girl should want to look good, this is the time when it really matters! Maybe if you dressed like the other girls, you'd get invited to some of their parties," her mother tried again.

MaryAnn shrugged her shoulders. Truthfully, she couldn't have cared less about either the clothes or the parties, and she really didn't understand what all the fuss was about.

What truly interested her was the new decorating scheme she was planning for her bedroom. The walls were already covered with posters of "sacred earth sites," places where MaryAnn and others in her web ring believed that the energies of the universe converged. She planned to set up displays in each of the four corners of her room featuring special crystals that had healing powers. And although she hadn't mentioned it to her mother yet, MaryAnn was making plans on-line to attend a special gathering at a remote location in the Canadian Rockies, where participants could experience the energies of the universe during the summer solstice.

According to the DSM-IV, the following are three typical features of schizotypal personality disorder: an ongoing pattern of interpersonal deficits, distorted or peculiar thinking, and eccentric behavior. These traits may show up as:

- odd or magical beliefs (superstitions; belief in telepathy or "sixth sense"; in children and adolescents, includes bizarre fantasies)
- odd thinking and speech
- bodily illusions
- suspiciousness or paranoid thinking
- feelings of alienation
- inappropriate emotional reaction to experiences
- odd, eccentric, or peculiar appearance or behavior
- no close friends beyond immediate family
- excessive social anxiety

The personality disorders in Cluster A are mainly characterized as eccentric, odd, or withdrawn. Schizotypal personality disorder is one of the most severe of the personality disorders; at times it appears similar to some stages of schizophrenia. It is considered by some to be as much a variant of schizophrenia as a personality disorder.

CLUSTER B PERSONALITY DISORDERS

Borderline personality disorder is one of the Cluster B disorders and is the only disorder in this category treated with psychiatric drugs. People with the disorders in Cluster B often appear to others as overly emotional, unstable, or self-dramatizing.

Borderline Personality Disorder

Henrietta's family never knew which side of her personality they would see next. One day her good mood was intense, and her positive opinion of herself seemed high. The next day her mood would be black as a thundercloud. She'd complain that she had no reason to live and that she couldn't stand the emptiness inside her any longer. Her sui-

An individual with borderline personality disorder may have difficulty communicating genuine feelings. He may express many sides to his personality, confusing those who are close to him.

A person with a borderline personality disorder may abuse al-cohol or other drugs.

cide threats were frequent, and some of her suicide attempts had come so close to succeeding that her family was very anxious.

Henrietta had no long-lasting friendships. She frequently made new friends very quickly, but then lost them just as quickly when people discovered how needy and demanding she could be. When her new friends stopped spending time with her, Henrietta responded with rage, telling everyone that she was victimized and neglected.

Henrietta secretly drank a great deal and frequently used recreational drugs. She knew that the alcohol and other drugs made her situation worse in the long run, but she couldn't seem to resist the escape they provided her—even if it was only temporary. She went on frequent shopping binges, charging her credit cards to the limit, then suffered a great deal of anxiety over how to pay her bills.

Borderline disorder is one of the most severe of the personality disorders. The word "borderline" is a designation that was originally used to indicate patients on the line between **neurosis** and **psychosis**, but now borderline personality disorder is recognized as a separate problem that is often associated with both neurotic and psychotic symptoms. According to the DSM-IV, the following are some of the typical features of borderline personality disorder: an ongoing pattern of instability in interpersonal relationships and self-image, and marked impulsivity. Traits that demonstrate these features may include:

- a frantic need to avoid abandonment (real or imagined)
- unstable and intense relationships with others, moving back and forth between extreme idealization and extreme devaluation
- impulsivity that could be damaging to self in: spending habits, sex, substance abuse, binge eating, reckless driving, and so on
- recurring suicide threats or attempts; self-mutilation
- unstable moods
- ongoing feelings of emptiness
- problems with anger
- *transient* psychotic episodes

In his book *PTSD/Borderlines in Therapy,* Jerome Kroll reports that a high percentage of people with borderline personality disorder turn out to have suffered abuse in childhood; he describes the myriad ways in which this abuse influences a patient's later life. These individuals often suffer from a disorder of the stream of consciousness:

an inability to turn off the stream of consciousness that has become its own enemy, comprised of actual memo-

ries of traumatic events, distorted and fragmented memories, intrusive imageries and flashbacks, dissociated memories, unwelcome somatic sensations, negative self-commentaries running like a ticker tape through the mind, fantasized and feared elaborations from childhood of abuse experiences, and concomitant strongly dysphoric mood of anxiety and anger.

A special feature of this personality disorder is that, according to the DSM-IV, the pattern of behavior seen in borderline personality disorder has been identified in many settings around the world. However, adolescents and young adults with identity problems (especially when accompanied by substance use) may temporarily display behaviors that give the false impression of borderline personality disorder. Teens often experience emotional ups and downs, as well as intense dilemmas about life choices—including sexual orientation and career choices—that can lead to anxiety and self-doubt. According to the DSM-IV, true borderline personality disorder is diagnosed predominantly (about 75 percent of all cases) in females.

CLUSTER C PERSONALITY DISORDERS

In the Cluster C category of personality disorders, both obsessive-compulsive and avoidant personality disorders may be treated with psychiatric drugs, though this treatment is not common. People with Cluster C personality disorders may appear tense and anxiety-ridden to others.

Obsessive-Compulsive Personality Disorder
Randall likes to tell people that he lives an orderly life. His alarm has been set at 5:30 for the past twenty-four and a

half years, but his wife has never been bothered by it because Randall quietly switches it off every morning at 5:29.

He slides out of bed without disturbing her, goes to the kitchen and turns on the coffeemaker. While he waits for his morning cup of naturally decaffeinated coffee to brew, he opens various bottles and takes out the thirteen vitamin and herbal supplements he will swallow later with his breakfast, lining them up on the counter according to size.

Randall leaves for work at 7:23, twenty minutes earlier than necessary, so that he will have those extra minutes to organize his desktop and credenza at the office, lining up pens and pencils in perfect order before he begins his workday.

He seldom goes to lunch with coworkers because he has so much reorganizing to do after his morning work. Also, the lunch hour is his time to check his daily to-do list and make sure he has ticked off several items by that time. He then calls his wife to see if she has completed the items he left on her to-do list as well.

Randall is a faithful, meticulous worker, but he is often late turning in projects because he feels the need to check, recheck, and sometimes check again every calculation he has made.

Family dinners end with each family member accounting for all the money he or she spent during the day. Randall records each figure in the family budget book. He goes to bed at 10:30 every evening, making sure before he shuts his eyes that his alarm, which hasn't been changed in years, is set for 5:30.

According to the DSM-IV, the following are some typical features of obsessive-compulsive personality disorder: inflexible attitudes; perfectionism; preoccupation with rules, details, and orderliness; and a rigid sense of morality. Traits that demonstrate these features may include:

- a preoccupation with details, lists, organization, or schedules that may cause the individual to lose sight of the major point of an activity
- perfectionism that interferes with completing a task
- devotion to work that excludes leisure time and friendships (this does not include excessive work that is due to financial necessity)
- inflexibility on matters of morality and ethics (not accounted for by cultural or religious identification)
- an inability to part with worn-out or worthless objects with no sentimental value
- a reluctance to delegate work or to work with others unless they do things his way
- rigidity and stubbornness
- money is seen as something to be hoarded against future catastrophes; has a miserly attitude toward spending

Avoidant Personality Disorder

Elijah wanted more than anything to have a friend. He had watched his high school classmates "hang" with their friends around their lockers and in the lunchroom, and heard some of them talk from time to time about their best friends. It sounded great to Elijah, but he had no idea of how to go about finding or making such a friend.

When the school counselor talked to Elijah, she asked him to tell her about his friends during elementary school. "Well," Elijah began hesitantly, "I can't really remember having any friends—not the kind you're probably talking about. My cousin came over sometimes for Sunday dinner and we played basketball while our parents talked."

"Oh," the counselor said, "so you and your cousin are good friends?"

Guidelines for Getting Psychiatric Drugs

1. Remember that only licensed professionals (medical doctors, advanced practice nurses, and pychiatrists) can prescribe medications.
2. If your therapist or primary care physician thinks you might benefit from a psychiatric medication, she can give you a referral to an appropriate licensed professional.
3. If you've gotten psychiatric drugs from your family doctor but your condition has not improved within a few weeks, see a psychiatrist. or advanced practice psychiatric nurse.
4. Your initial appointment with a psychiatrist or advanced practice psychiatric nurse should allow enough time to explain all your symptoms. The first visit typically lasts from fifty to sixty minutes.
5. The psychiatrist should be able to explain the reasons why he or she is prescribing a particular drug for you.
6. Always feel free to get a second opinion.
7. Before you take the medicine, make sure you understand the possible side effects, how long the medication takes to become effective, what to do if you miss a dose, what the risks and benefits of the medicine are, and what alternative treatments are available.
8. Depending on your individual situation, you may want to consider involving your family in your treatment and your appointments. They may be able to offer a unique perspective on your situation or offer symptoms that you may not have noticed.
9. Follow-up visits are essential. When you first start the medication, you may need to be seen weekly, but once you have found the right medication for you, you will probably go for less frequent maintenance visits.

Adapted from Jack M. Gorman, M.D.'s *The Essential Guide to Psychiatric Drugs.*

"Yeah, I guess you could say that," Elijah said. "Except he's ten years older than me, so he's away at med school now, and I don't see him much anymore."

"What about friends your own age, Elijah? Did you have any while you were in elementary school?"

Elijah shook his head back and forth.

"How about when you were in kindergarten?"

He shook his head again.

"Did you ever get involved in any clubs or organizations? Boy Scouts, maybe?"

"No. I don't do things like that," he answered.

"Why not?"

Elijah shrugged and didn't answer for several seconds. At last he tried to explain. "When you go to things like that—Boy Scouts, I mean—sometimes the other people don't want you there. I mean, you have to be able to *do* things, you know? Like they all can. Tie knots and go hiking and all that kind of stuff."

"And you can't?"

He shrugged again. "I'd just make a fool of myself. They'd all laugh at me."

As the counselor and Elijah had more conversations in the following weeks, information about his home life began to surface. From the earliest time he could remember, even before he went to kindergarten, Elijah's parents had criticized Elijah constantly. Nothing he did or said was ever good enough to win his parents' approval. After a while, he realized he was "different," not as good as other kids his age, and he stopped trying. He'd retreated into his own safe little world, avoiding any activity that could bring criticism or scorn; he'd been there ever since.

According to the DSM-IV, the following are some of the typical features of avoidant personality disorder: an ongoing pattern of being socially inhibited; feelings of inadequacy; and extreme sensitivity to what other people think of them. Traits that demonstrate these features may include:

- unwillingness to get involved with others unless certain of being liked
- restraint in intimate relationships due to fear of shame or ridicule
- preoccupation with criticism or rejection in social situations
- inhibition in new interpersonal situations due to feelings of inadequacy
- seeing self as socially inept, personally unappealing, or inferior to others
- reluctance to engage in new activities for fear of being embarrassed
- avoidance of jobs that entail interpersonal contact for fear of being criticized or rejected

An individual with avoidant personality disorder may be preoccupied with social rejection.

PSYCHIATRIC DRUG THERAPY

Psychiatric drugs are not usually the first or the most important treatment for personality disorders. Different types of psychotherapy are routinely used for patients with these disorders (for more information, see chapter five on treatment). However, each of the personality disorders described in this chapter can also be treated in at least some measure with psychiatric medications.

Antipsychotic Drugs

These drugs, such as haloperidol (Haldol), are used to treat patients with paranoid personality disorder who are having brief psychotic episodes. Individuals with borderline personality disorder or schizotypal personality disorder are also given antipsychotic medications, though low doses are used in such cases.

Antidepressants and Antianxiety Medications

Antidepressants are used often in the treatment of patients with borderline personality disorder, and occasionally in the treatment of those with schizoid personality disorder. When patients with avoidant personality disorder also have a social phobia (see another book in this series, *Drug Therapy and Anxiety Disorders*, for more information on social phobia), they may benefit from treatment with one of the monoamine oxidase inhibitor (MAOI) antidepressants.

However, since MAOIs have serious side effects, they are not typically prescribed these days. Instead, antidepressant medications called selective serotonin reuptake inhibitors (SSRIs) may be more useful to relieve depression and irritability in patients with borderline personality disorder. Some of the SSRIs are approved by the FDA for personality disorders, while others are used "off-label." Examples of useful SSRIs include fluoxetine (Prozac), sertraline (Zoloft), and paroxetine HCl (Paxil).

Mood Stabilizers

Carbamazepine (Tegretol) is prescribed to treat patients with borderline personality disorder who experience outbursts of rage and other behavioral problems. Lithium and divalproex sodium (Depakote) are also used.

Potentially Addictive Medications

Professional mental health workers caution that medications with the potential to be addictive should not be used in the treatment of patients with borderline personality disorder.

SUMMARY

Although psychiatric drugs are used in conjunction with different types of therapy, in some cases, medication can aid in the treatment of patients with personality disorders. Psychiatric drugs can help calm the most troublesome symptoms, so that the individual can begin to deal with emotional issues through counseling and other forms of therapy.

Alcohol is one of the substances used most frequently by human beings to alter their mental state.

3 | Psychiatric Drugs in History

Using drugs that alter the mental state has been a common practice for thousands of years. Alcohol, opiates, cocaine, and peyote are some of the drugs most commonly used for this purpose. These drugs are thought to change behavior by acting on the brain systems that govern behaviors such as sleeping, eating, and sexual behavior. For centuries, people saw the effects of such drugs but had little or no idea of how or why the drugs produced their effects. As researchers and medical health professionals continue to study the brain and its systems, they are gaining more and more insight into how psychiatric drugs work.

For example, reference to a medicine made from the plant Rauwolfia serpentina can be found in Ayurmedic texts of India that are more than two thousand years old. This medicine was used to treat symptoms similar to those of schizophrenia and bipolar disorder. Reserpine was probably the active ingredient in this medicine, but it was not until the 1930s that this ingredient was isolated and studied. It was then used to treat psychotic disorders in the 1950s, and did so effectively.

Lithium is a drug often prescribed today for individuals with bipolar disorder. Writings from the time of the Roman Empire recommended that patients with *mania* use water from specific alkaline springs, water that most likely contained lithium. Plant preparations containing opium have been used to treat pain for hundreds of years, and in the last two centuries, derivatives of these plants were used to treat psychotic disorders and depression. Coca leaves, which are the source of cocaine, were used around the beginning of the twentieth century as a *stimulant* and antidepressant. The famous psychologist Sigmund Freud chewed coca leaves.

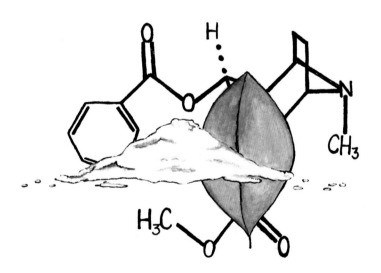

Coca leaves contain a chemical that acts as a stimulant and antidepressant.

Some hallucinogens are made from certain kinds of mushrooms.

MODERN DRUG DISCOVERIES AND DEVELOPMENT

The treatment of many physical ailments was changed dramatically by Sir Alexander Fleming's discovery of antibiotics in 1928, and Jonas Edward Salk's development of a polio vaccine in the mid-1950s. Now the treatment of many psychiatric ailments is also being changed dramatically by the discovery and development of new drugs that alter mood, behavior, and mental functioning. Help is now available for mental disorders that were considered untreatable just a few decades ago.

Between the early 1900s and the mid-1900s, severe mental illness in America increased to such an extent that the numbers of people institutionalized in mental hospitals grew from two out of a thousand people to four out of a thousand. There was little treatment available to help such patients, however, and they were routinely "warehoused" in state institutions. The most popular psychiatric treatments at the time were electric shock or various psychotherapies. No one considered drugs to be a treatment option for mental illness.

However, one surgeon in Paris who was working to find a way to reduce surgical shock in his patients began a whole new interest in psychiatric drugs. In 1952, this surgeon, Henri Laborit, noticed that when he gave his patients a strong dose of **antihistamines**, they became much less anxious about their upcoming surgery and could therefore be sedated with less anesthetic. This had the exact effect Laborit had been searching for—it reduced surgical shock in his patients. Laborit did not stop there, however.

When he observed how strongly the antihistamine chlorpromazine hydrochloride (Thorazine) affected his patients' mental state, he began to think that these drugs might have another use—in the field of psychiatry. When psychiatrist Pierre Deniker tried chlorpromazine with his most agitated and uncontrollable patients, the results were amazing. Patients who had needed to be restrained because of their violent behavior could now be left without supervision. Patients who had stood in one spot without moving for weeks could now respond to other people. It was a long and difficult struggle to get medical professionals to consider treating mental disorders with a drug, but eventually medical professionals began to try chlorpromazine in state institutions, and once again the results seemed miraculous.

GLOSSARY

antihistamines: Chemicals that block the production of histamine in the body and are used in the treatment of allergies.

Brand Names vs. Generic Names

Talking about psychiatric drugs can be confusing, because every drug has at least two names: its "generic name" and the "brand name" that the pharmaceutical company uses to market the drug. Generic names come from the drugs' chemical structures, while brand names are used by drug companies in order to inspire public recognition and loyalty for their products.

Here are the brand names and generic names for some common psychiatric drugs:

Depakote®	valproate
Haldol®	haloperidol
Librium®	chlordiazepoxide
Eskalith®,	lithium
Lithobid®, and	
Lithonate®	
Paxil®	paroxetine
Prozac®	fluoxetine
Norpramin®	desipramine
Sinequan®	doxepin
Tegretol®	carbamazepine
Thorazine®	chlorpromazine
Tofranil®	imipramine
Valium®	diazepam
Xanax®	alprazolam
Zoloft®	sertraline hydrochloride

G L O S S A R Y

hallucinations: Sensory perceptions with no basis in reality.

delusions: False beliefs based on an incorrect perception of reality.

sedating: Having a calming, soothing effect.

When the U.S. Food and Drug Administration approved chlorpromazine in 1954, the drug had a tremendous effect on people with mental disorders, decreasing the intensity of schizophrenia symptoms such as *hallucinations* and *delusions*. It calmed people without *sedating* them and, in many cases, allowed them to lead almost normal lives. By 1964, fifty million people around the world had taken the drug.

Drug Approval

Before a drug can be marketed in the United States, it must be officially approved by the Food and Drug Administration (FDA). Today's FDA is the primary consumer protection agency in the United States. Operating under the authority given it by the government, and guided by laws established throughout the twentieth century, the FDA has established a rigorous drug approval process that verifies the safety, effectiveness, and accuracy of labeling for any drug marketed in the United States.

While the United States has the FDA for the approval and regulation of drugs and medical devices, Canada has a similar organization called the Therapeutic Product Directorate (TPD). The TPD is a division of Health Canada, the Canadian government department of health. The TPD regulates drugs, medical devices, disinfectants, and sanitizers with disinfectant claims. Some of the things that the TPD monitors are quality, effectiveness, and safety. Just as the FDA must approve new drugs in the United States, the TPD must approve new drugs in Canada before those drugs can enter the market.

Drugs Used In History

Drug use, whether medicinal or recreational, is not solely a modern pheno-menon. Following are some of the substances that have been used throughout history:

ANCIENT WORLD

alcohol	cannabis (marijuana or
opium	related substance)
hemlock	atropine (from nightshade
	or belladonna plants)

MIDDLE AGES

alcohol	liquors
opium	

AGE OF EXPLORATION

alcohol	coca
coffee (caffeine)	tobacco (nicotine)

1800s

cocaine	morphine (an opium derivative)
heroin	amphetamines
ether	curare

1900s

peyote	ecstasy
LSD	PCP (angel dust)

Adapted from *A Brief History of Psychopharmacology* by Dr. C. George Boeree.

Side effects are often considered a negative aspect of drug use. But one of the side effects associated with chlorpromazine—effects similar to those of Parkinson's disease—had positive effects in that it made researchers begin to think differently about brain function and behavior.

They reasoned that if a chemical substance, such as chlorpromazine, could produce effects similar to those of Parkinson's disease, then perhaps similar chemicals found in the brain might be involved in producing actual Parkinson's disease. They began to study the possibility of counteracting these chemicals. This new way of thinking about chemicals in the brain eventually resulted in understanding the role of dopamine and other **neurotransmitters**, an advance that has had great impact on the treatment of mental disorders. (See chapter four for an explanation of how neurotransmitters work in the central nervous system.)

When antipsychotics like chlorpromazine relieved psychotic symptoms such as hallucinations and delusions, researchers discovered that these effects were due to the drugs' ability to block dopamine receptors in the brain. As a result, scientists began to explore the possibility that schizophrenia could be caused by an excess of dopamine.

Researchers later discovered the relationship between depression and a lack of the neurotransmitters serotonin and noradrenaline. Operating on the same principle, they investigated to see if anxiety could be caused by a lack of GABA (a neurotransmitter called gamma-aminobutyric acid).

As researchers and medical professionals gained this new and ever-growing understanding of how medications affect the brain, more and more psychiatric drugs were developed. Chlorpromazine was followed by other antipsychotics—both standard antipsychotics and, decades later, the newer atypical antipsychotics. Some of the antipsy-

GLOSSARY

neurotransmitters: *Chemicals found in the brain that aid the transmission of impulses across the gaps between nerve cells.*

chotics are now used to treat people with paranoid, border-line, and schizotypal personality disorders.

Other classes of drugs aimed at other types of mental disorders followed. The benzodiazepines (such as Valium and Xanax) were developed in the late 1950s and proved to be very effective in treating anxiety. However, drugs in the benzodiazepine class also had the potential to be addictive and had many side effects. Research continued for drugs that could produce the same positive effects without the drawbacks.

Some of the antidepressant drugs, MAOIs, were discovered in the course of tuberculosis treatment. When tuberculosis patients were given an antibiotic called iproniazide, those who were also depressed experienced relief from their depression. The same medication helped alleviate problems the patients had with appetite, energy, and sleep. When investigative studies were done, iproniazide was shown to produce these effects by inhibiting the *enzyme* called mono-amine oxidase. This sets in motion a process leading to a higher concentration of neurotransmitters called the mono-amines (norepinephrine, serotonin, and dopamine) in the brain, thus helping relieve depression. (See chapter four for more details on how different classes of drugs work.) Because iproniazide was so successful in treating depression, more drugs of the MAOI type were developed. Today, MAOIs are sometimes used for patients with avoidant personality disorder who also have social phobia. However, MAOIs have potential serious side effects, and they require strict dietary restrictions, so they are not the first choice for treatment.

In the last half of the twentieth century, while researchers were searching for more drugs to use in treating psychotic disorders, they observed that one of the compounds they tested seemed to help depressed patients sub-

> **GLOSSARY**
>
> **enzyme:** A complex protein produced by living cells that causes specific biochemical reactions.

stantially. This compound, imipramine (Tofranil), the first of the tricyclic antidepressants (TCAs), has been a highly successful antidepressant and is still used today, not only to treat depression but also obsessive-compulsive disorder, *Tourette's disorder*, *bulimia nervosa*, and avoidant personality disorder. Given the success of imipramine, researchers went on to develop many more drugs in this class.

In the 1980s, pharmaceutical companies began working on a new class of antidepressants that would have fewer side effects than the TCAs. They designed a new class of drugs that blocked the reuptake of serotonin, but not norepinephrine, and called them selective serotonin reuptake inhibitors (SSRIs). The first of these drugs was called fluoxetine (Prozac). Several other SSRIs were then developed that have also been successful, including sertraline (Zoloft) and paroxetine (Paxil). These antidepressants are now used, among other things, to help patients with schizoid personality disorder manage their anxiety and to relieve depression and irritability in patients with borderline personality disorder. The SSRIs are usually the first choice for treatment, since they have less potential for serious side effects, and they do not require the cardiac and laboratory monitoring that TCAs need.

INSIDE THE BRAIN

Understanding how psychiatric drugs work inside the brain helps medical professionals know which medications to prescribe for which disorder. It also provides researchers with important information for developing new drugs. But this information is not always easy to obtain. While it is relatively simple to tell what is going on in other body organs by means of a blood test, information about the brain is

GLOSSARY

Tourette's disorder: *A disorder characterized by involuntary motor and/or vocal tics.*

bulimia nervosa: *An eating disorder in which periods of binge eating are followed by purging, the misuse of laxatives or diuretics, and other methods of controlling weight.*

harder to come by. Many medicines are not able to even get into the brain because of what scientists refer to as the *blood–brain barrier*.

However, advances in imaging techniques have helped solve some of the problems with "seeing" inside the brain. With the development of these latest techniques, scientists can now inject chemicals labeled with tiny amounts of radioactivity into a person's bloodstream. They can then watch where the chemicals go inside the brain and what receptors they bind to. The most commonly used imaging techniques include:

- CAT (computerized axial tomography) scans—reveals brain structures without harming the patient
- MRI (magnetic resonance imaging)—gives highly refined pictures of the brain using magnetic fields, and without using radiation
- PET (positron emission tomography) and SPECT (single-photon emission computed tomography)—reveal brain structure and also show metabolic activity in various parts of the brain (brain chemicals and their receptors)

While scientists are making great strides with these techniques, at this point, tools like these can only be used to help researchers learn more about psychiatric disorders and to develop appropriate treatment strategies. The various imaging techniques are not yet perfect enough to be able to be used as psychiatric diagnostic tools. In other words, scientists cannot yet look at a picture of an individual's brain and determine the exact psychiatric problem. Much about the brain remains a mystery—but researchers are hopeful that in the future, imaging techniques will be used to confirm psychiatric diagnoses the same way they are used today for medical conditions.

GENETIC RESEARCH

Research on ways to treat mental disorders continues on other fronts as well. With the advent of genetic research, molecular geneticists have been able to link some psychiatric diseases, such as schizophrenia and bipolar disorder, to abnormal genes. Many research studies are being conducted currently to identify specific markers on genes that transmit psychiatric disorders from generation to generation. This research will provide scientists with important information for identifying people at risk of developing a pschiatric disorder, and it will also make possible early diagnosis and treatment. Genetic research can also help scientists understand if certain subtypes of psychiatric disorders run together, requiring different treatment strategies from those that occur alone.

OTHER RESEARCH

Researchers have developed other methods to study psychotheapies under controlled conditions. Many studies now compare psychotherapeutic interventions (such as different types of counseling therapy) to medication. This means that the outcome of psychotherapies can now be compared scientifically to the outcome of medication treatment, allowing practitioners to gain a better understanding of the uses and limitations of both types of treatment.

SUMMARY

Researchers and medical professionals have been quick to observe the effects of psychiatric drugs and to suggest new and broader uses for them. Research in this field is ongoing, with new drugs being developed and tested continually. Psychiatric medications, often used in conjunction with other treatment, can make a tremendous difference in the life of many people diagnosed with personality disorders.

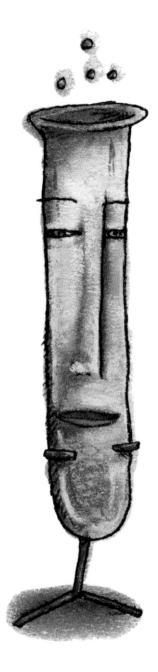

Psychiatric drugs are made from chemicals that affect the way brain cells behave. Scientists have developed these chemicals after years of research.

4 | How Psychiatric Drugs Work

Psychiatric drugs do their work unseen, deep inside the brain. These chemicals can change the firing patterns of neural circuits and the tone of neural activity in the brain. By doing so, they can change some of the aspects of consciousness that make us most human.

The brain has long been a mystery and a source of amazement. Slowly, year after year, researchers have continued their work to uncover these mysteries. We now have a partial picture of how the brain operates, though there is still far more to learn. A basic understanding of how the brain operates is necessary to understand how psychiatric medications can help in the treatment of mental disorders.

The brain contains multiple millions of specialized brain cells called neurons. In fact, there are so many neurons in our brains that if all the neurons with their axons from a single human brain were stretched out end to end, they would go to the moon and back.

Neurons are highly specialized cells that pass messages between them, and they are not found only in the brain. The central nervous system (CNS), which includes the spinal cord, also contains neurons, both sensory and motor. Our five senses—sight, hearing, smell, touch, and taste—feed information from the outside world to the brain by way of these sensory neurons. Motor neurons then respond to this information by making the muscles of our bodies move.

When we face danger or experience certain kinds of pain, our motor and sensory neurons work together to move us out of harm's way. For instance, if a man hammering a

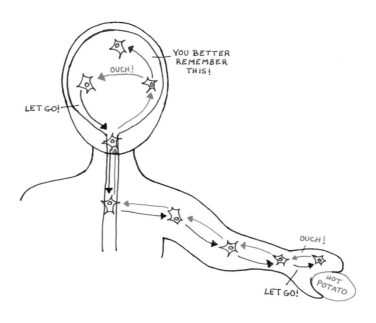

If we were to pick up a hot potato, nerves would carry messages to the brain and back again—and the brain would learn a valuable lesson for the future!

nail into a board accidentally hits his finger instead of the nail, sensory neurons relay that information from neuron to neuron until it reaches the spinal cord. There, information is sent back to the finger, telling it to move out of harm's way. All of this happens in the blink of an eye or less, while at the same time information about the dangers of using a hammer is being stored in the man's memory so that he will exercise caution the next time he uses one.

Neurons are uniquely designed to do their job, which is to carry messages. Each neuron has a cell body, and from that center, it sends out dendrites and axons. Dendrites are projections that look a little like tiny twigs. Axons are long, thin filaments; several terminal buttons lie on the dendrites, so that each neuron functions as a link in the communication chain. This is not a chain that runs in only one direction, however. Each neuron is in contact with many other neurons, making the CNS into a vast mesh or web of interconnected groups of neurons. The communication interconnections between these millions of neurons—with their cell bodies, axons, and dendrites—is the information superhighway of the human body.

Brain cells communicate by sending electrical signals from neuron to neuron. While the axons and dendrites are very close together, they do not actually touch other neurons. In between is a tiny space called a synapse. Nerve impulses travel through this synapse, jumping the space in much the same way an electrical current would. When a message is to be transferred, a neuron "fires," and its terminal buttons release chemicals called neurotransmitters (biochemical substances such as norepinephrine and dopamine), which make jumping the synapse possible. When an electrical signal comes to the end of one neuron, the cell fires, secreting the proper neurotransmitter into the synapse. This chemical messenger then crosses from

the presynaptic neuron (the brain cell sending the message) to the postsynaptic neuron (the brain cell receiving the message), where it binds itself to the appropriate chemical receptor and influences the behavior of this second neuron.

When the neurotransmitter binds to the receptors, other processes are set in motion in the postsynaptic brain cell, either exciting it to keep sending the message along or *inhibiting* it to stop the transmission of the message. After the impulse is passed from one neuron to another, the neurotransmitter falls off the receptor and back into the synapse. There it is either taken back up into the presynaptic neuron (a kind of neuron recycling), broken down by enzymes and discarded to spinal fluid surrounding the brain, or reattached to the receptor, thus strengthening the original signal that was sent from the presynaptic neuron.

The brain has at least one hundred billion synapses. Researchers speculate that there may be hundreds of different neurotransmitters. And many neurons respond to more than one neurotransmitter. Within this complex brain environment psychiatric drugs operate, usually by influencing the neurotransmitters.

Psychiatric drugs appear to act on systems built into the brain to regulate behaviors like eating, sleeping, and sexual activity. These drugs come in from the outside, like invading soldiers, and take over the body's normal processes, altering states of arousal, attention, emotional state, and thinking.

CLASSES OF DRUGS AND THEIR ACTIONS

Different classes of drugs operate in different ways inside the brain. The classes of drugs used to treat personality dis-

---

Neurotransmitters and Mental Disorders

Neurotransmitter	Related Mental Disorders
dopamine	schizophrenia; drug addiction
norepinephrine	mood disorders; anxiety disorders
beta-endorphin	drug addiction
serotonin	mood disorders
gamma-aminobutyric acid	anxiety disorders

---

orders include antipsychotics, mood stabilizers, and antidepressants (TCAs, SSRIs, and MAOIs).

Antipsychotics

Most psychiatric drugs get their power from their ability to influence the tiny space between nerve cells, the synapse. In one way or another, they affect neurotransmitters binding to receptors. The antipsychotic drugs—drugs that treat psychotic symptoms like hallucinations and delusions—block the ability of the neurotransmitter dopamine to bind to the dopamine receptor. Therefore, when a nerve signal reaches the end of a neuron that uses dopamine as its neurotransmitter, the presynaptic neuron secretes dopamine into the synapse, but the "keyhole"—the receptor—is blocked by the antipsychotic drug. The dopamine is then taken apart by enzymes; some is taken back up into the presynaptic neuron, but it never gets to do its job, and so the neural signal cannot keep traveling from neuron to neuron. Thorazine, Haldol, Prolixin, and Mellaril are all examples of this kind of drug. Haloperidol (Haldol) is now used to treat patients with paranoid personality disorder who are having brief psychotic episodes.

Mood Stabilizers

Mood stabilizers such as carbamazepine (Tegretol) work in many different ways in the brain. They affect receptors, neurotransmitter concentrations, and *ion channels*—but researchers still don't know which one of these actions stabilizes mood.

Antidepressants

The antidepressants used to treat schizoid and borderline personality disorders include TCAs, SSRIs, and MAOIs.

TCAs seem to produce their effects by operating on the monoamine neurotransmitters. They block the reuptake of norepinephrine into presynaptic neurons; in other words, they inhibit the uptake of norepinephrine back into the cells that released it. They appear to act in a similar but weaker way on serotonin, and they have little effect on dopamine. Because they block the reuptake of these neurotransmitters, TCAs actually increase the amount of serotonin and norepinephrine available to brain receptors. These neurotransmitters are vital for many functions and have been related to depression, anger, and impulsivity.

Like the TCAs, drugs in the SSRI class increase the amount of certain neurotransmitters available to brain receptors. SSRIs usually work with fewer side effects than do some of the TCAs. As the name of this class of drugs suggest, SSRIs work by specifically inhibiting the reuptake of serotonin, thus making more of this vital neurotransmitter available in the brain. They do not block the reuptake of norepinephrine, however, which is why they are called "selective." The SSRIs that are used to treat patients with borderline personality disorder for depression and irritability include fluoxetine (Prozac), sertraline (Zoloft), and paroxetine (Paxil).

MAOIs inhibit monoamine oxidase, an enzyme that breaks down dopamine, epinephrine, norepinephrine, and

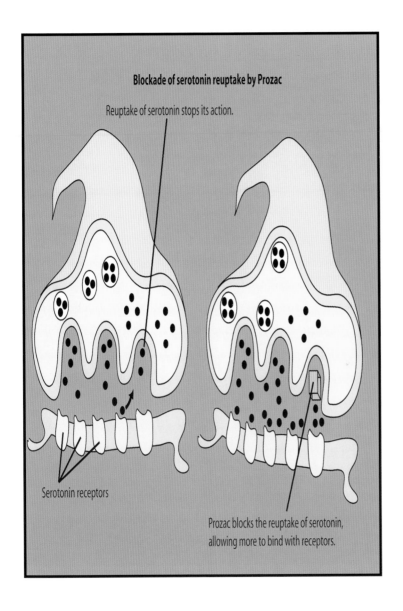

Blockade of serotonin reuptake by Prozac

Reuptake of serotonin stops its action.

Serotonin receptors

Prozac blocks the reuptake of serotonin, allowing more to bind with receptors.

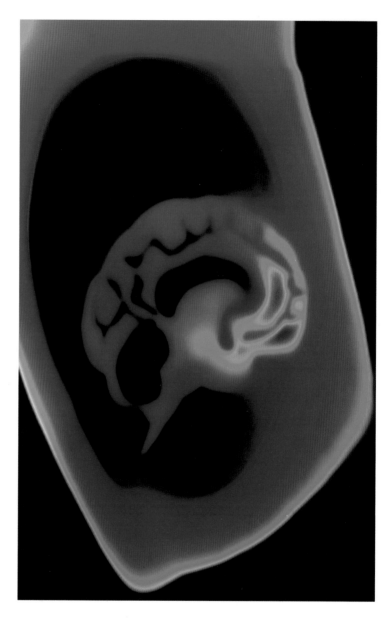

The human brain is a mysterious and complicated organ.

serotonin. The drug results in higher levels of these neuro-transmitters, which are used as chemical messengers in the brain.

Atypical Neuroleptics (Atypical Antipsychotics)

These drugs are the new generation of antipsychotic medication. They are usually considered first-line medications for people who experience psychotic episodes; in other words, medical practitioners prescribe them first before they try one of the older antipsychotic medications. The atypical neuroleptics have fewer and less serious side effects. They are effective for treating mood instability and paranoia, as well as psychosis.

SUMMARY

The brain is a fascinating organ, and many patients now benefit from the intensive research that continues regarding how it operates. As researchers and mental health professionals uncover more and more information about the ways in which psychiatric medications affect the brain, an increasing number of patients will receive helpful treatment for their personality disorders and other mental disorders.

A person with a personality disorder may resist medical treatment. Even if he does consult a doctor or other practitioner, he may refuse to believe there is anything wrong with him.

5 | Treatment Description

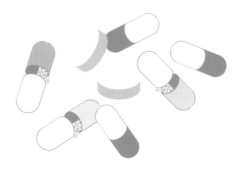

Personality disorders are often treated with one of several forms of psychotherapy, including ***cognitive-behavioral*** therapy, group therapy, or family therapy, combined with ***pharmacotherapy*** when appropriate.

Getting an individual with a personality disorder to go to a medical professional can be very difficult, because in most cases the individual feels that he doesn't have a problem. The traits that are causing trouble in his life may even seem normal, or ego-syntonic, to him. Such a person may say, "This is just the way I am." Because of this, people with personality disorders do not usually seek help unless their families put pressure on them to do so, or unless they get into trouble with the law.

An advanced practice nurse has been trained to prescribe and administer medications.

Advanced Practice Psychiatric Nurses

Doctors and psychiatrists aren't the only ones who can diagnose and treat psychiatric disorders. As part of their training, advanced practice psychiatric nurses complete coursework and internships in psychiatry—both therapy and psychopharmocology (the study of medicines)—as well as the medical training required for nursing. After their training is completed, these practitioners are certified and licensed as either psychiatric clinical nurse specialists or nurse practitioners. They can prescribe and administer medications, just like a doctor or psychiatrist.

PSYCHIATRY AND PERSONALITY DISORDERS

Psychiatry is the name of the medical specialty that diagnoses, treats, and works to prevent disorders of the mind. Psychiatrists are medical doctors who complete a ***residency*** in psychiatry. Because they are physicians, psychiatrists can also prescribe and administer drugs. Advance practice psychiatric nurses can also diagnose psychiatric disorders and prescribe and administer drug treatment.

The basis for good treatment of any mental disorder is an accurate diagnosis. In the treatment of personality disorders, physicians have no specific tests they can perform to make their diagnoses conclusively. Instead, information about the patient must be gathered from several different sources. This information will include the length of time the patient has experienced difficulties, what areas of her life are affected, and to what degree. To this end, the psychiatrist may begin by using one or more clinical interviews as a basic diagnostic technique. During the interviews, the psychiatrist not only listens to the patient's words, but also observes carefully many nonverbal signals, such as how the patient is dressed and groomed, body language, and eye contact. Because patients with personality disorders may not be aware of how their behavior impacts others, the psychiatrist may also speak with family members, friends, or co-workers to form a more accurate assessment of the patient's condition.

Another tool commonly used in diagnosing personality disorders is testing. Both intelligence and personality tests or inventories may be used and both are usually administered by a clinical psychologist. The personality inventory allows health care professionals to obtain information that is sometimes difficult to get from an interview with the patient. The most widely used inventory is the Minnesota Mul-

GLOSSARY

residency: A period of not less than one year and often three to seven years of postgraduate training for health care professionals.

When Psychiatric Medicines May Be Needed

When a patient exhibits:

- suicidal thoughts
- the presence of hallucinations or delusions
- a decrease in the ability to function (includes inability to sleep, eat, work, care for children, perform personal hygiene)
- self-destructive behavior
- uncontrollable compulsions (constant washing or checking)

---

tiphasic Personality Inventory, first developed in the 1930s for use with hospital inpatients. The MMPI has been updated and restandardized. It now consists of 567 questions in which an individual is asked to rate each statement about himself as being mainly true or mainly false.

PSYCHOTHERAPY

Psychoanalysis

Psychotherapy can take several different forms. Psychoanalysis, the "talking cure," was first developed by Sigmund Freud. In this form of psychotherapy, the patient talks at length about her own life and experiences, with the psychoanalyst offering interpretations when appropriate.

Psychodynamic Therapy

Psychodynamic therapy has been used in the treatment of all of the personality disorders but particularly with the most severe types. This therapy, in which the therapist focuses on the patient's problems in the present rather than trying to relate her problems to experiences in her childhood, is proving valuable in treating individuals with borderline personality disorder. Unlike psychoanalysis, psychodynamic sessions do not explore the patient's past in great depth, even though the therapist must have a detailed account of her childhood. Instead, expressive psychotherapy, developed by Dr. Otto Kernberg, allows the patient–therapist relationship to grow to the point where the patient will eventually "act out" her conflicts toward the therapist. At that point, the therapist is able to verbally confront the patient's emotional and behavioral inconsistencies. Psychodynamic therapy usually takes place at least twice a week and continues for several years.

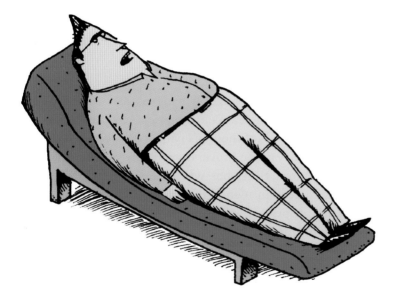

Sigmund Freud developed the "talking cure." Freud's patients reclined on a couch and described their lives in detail.

Cognitive therapy offers an "umbrella" from emotional storms.

Cognitive Therapy

Other forms of therapy include cognitive therapy, in which dysfunctional thinking patterns can be addressed through methods such as confrontation, persuasion, and by reshaping the kinds of thoughts patients entertain. A professor of psychiatry at the University of Pennsylvania School of Medicine, Aaron Beck, has written extensively about how people with certain mental disorders, such as anxiety and depression, appraise their situation in a dysfunctional way. This type of thinking can, at least in part, actually help the person to stay both anxious and depressed. Catastrophic thinking, one of Beck's examples, is a type of dysfunctional thinking in which people dwell on the worst outcome possible. Beck developed cognitive therapy, which is short term, problem oriented, and primarily educational, to help people change the mistaken ways they look at their situations.

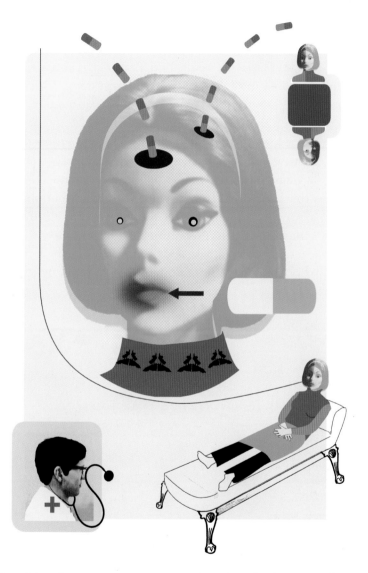

Cognitive therapy, sometimes combined with pharmacotherapy, can teach an individual to think and speak differently about her circumstances, thereby shaping her reality in more positive ways.

Behavior Therapy

Behavior therapy focuses on a patient's problem behavior and ways to change it. Different behavioral techniques include systematic desensitization, flooding, relaxation techniques, and impulse control training. In systematic desensitization, a patient faces difficult situations gradually, from least difficult to most difficult. (For instance, someone who is afraid of spiders might first simply look at pictures of spiders, then watch movies about spiders, and finally be exposed to actual spiders.) Flooding is a technique that requires the patient to face the most difficult situation first, often with the support of the therapist. Relaxation techniques may include deep-breathing exercises, muscle relaxation exercises and tapes, and biofeedback. When people feel anxious, their bodies automatically respond by tensing

Behavior therapy helps people retreat to a calm, safe state of mind whenever they face anxiety-producing circumstances.

muscles, and these exercises and techniques can help people maintain a calm feeling when they face situations that formerly produced anxiety. Behavior therapy that includes impulse control training can be very helpful for patients with borderline personality disorder.

Group Therapy

Group therapy has proven useful in some cases of schizoid personality disorder, since peer pressure from other members of the group can provide the motivation needed to change. Interacting with a group can help patients learn new ways to manage their symptoms and can also help patients meet and begin to interact with new people. Because personality disorders can cause problems among families, family therapy is one positive way in which this issue can be addressed.

Psychotherapy for patients with personality disorders is often a long-term treatment. For those with borderline personality disorders, therapy may need to continue for a decade or more.

Most personality disorders can be treated on an outpatient basis, but hospitalization can be an important part of treatment for patients with borderline personality disorder who threaten to commit suicide or who are going through withdrawal from alcohol or drugs. It may also be needed for individuals with paranoid personality disorder who are experiencing psychotic symptoms.

When Psychotherapy Is Not Appropriate

Specific types of psychotherapy are not appropriate for all patients with personality disorders. Psychoanalytic psychotherapy is not considered appropriate for patients who

When Either Psychiatric Medicines or Psychotherapy May Work

When a patient exhibits:

- depression that does not include suicidal thoughts, loss of function or inability to eat or sleep
- panic disorder
- generalized anxiety disorder
- social phobia
- bulimia

---

suffer from paranoid personality disorders. In *Personality Disorders*, Rebecca J. Frey states that such patients are "likely to resent the therapist and see him or her as trying to control or dominate them."

Often personality disorders are treated with psychotherapy alone. In some cases, however, pharmacotherapy is also indicated.

PHARMACOTHERAPY

In the case of some mental disorders, psychiatric drugs provide great relief, even alleviating the majority of symptoms. This is not usually the case with personality disorders, however.

This is not to say, however, that drug therapies are of *no* value in treating personality disorders. Psychiatric drugs, used under the supervision of knowledgeable doctors and usually in conjunction with one of the psychotherapies, can provide much help to patients with selected personality disorders.

Psychiatric drugs cannot cure personality disorders, but they can alleviate some of the emotional symptoms.

Paranoid Personality Disorder

Patients with paranoid personality disorder sometimes experience brief psychotic episodes, in which they have a temporary break with reality. In these cases, antipsychotic drugs such as haloperidol (Haldol) can be effective in treating the psychotic episodes. Therapists have also used antidepressants, such as imipramine hydrochloride (Tofranil), desipramine hydrochloride (Norpramin), and doxepin hydrochloride (Sinequan); and antianxiety drugs such as chlordiazepoxide hydrochloride (Librium) and diazepam (Valium) for this purpose. Atypical neuroleptics such as Risperdal, Zyprexa, or Geodone are also used.

Schizotypal Personality Disorder

Some patients with schizotypal personality disorder are given low doses of antipsychotic drugs such as haloperidol (Haldol), but the effectiveness of this treatment is still not completely proven.

Borderline Personality Disorder

Patients with borderline personality disorder may experience outbursts of rage. For such outbursts, mood stabilizers such as carbamazepine (Tegretol) may be helpful. Carbamazepine is also used to treat other behavioral problems in these patients. Valproate (Depakote) can be used as a mood stabilizer for this personality disorder, as can lithium. There is mounting evidence that SSRI medications such as fluoxetine (Prozac), sertraline (Zoloft), and paroxetine (Paxil) can relieve depression and irritability for borderline personality disorder patients in some cases.

Avoidant Personality Disorder

Individuals with avoidant personality disorder often suffer from *phobias* and *panic attacks* as well, particularly social phobia (see another book in this series, *Anxiety Disor-*

GLOSSARY

phobias: Fears brought on by the presence or anticipation of some thing or situation.

panic attacks: Periods of extreme fear, with the development of symptoms such as fear of dying, going crazy, or losing control. These symptoms reach their peak within 10 minutes. Other symptoms may include tightening in the chest, shortness of breath, dizziness, and fainting.

ders, for more information on social phobia). To treat these phobias and panic attacks, antipsychotic drugs such as haloperidol (Haldol) can be effective. Sometimes therapists also use antidepressants, such as imipramine (Tofranil), desipramine (Norpramin), and doxepin (Sinequan); and antianxiety drugs such as chlordiazepoxide (Librium) and diazepam (Valium). The SSRIs are also very effective for treating this disorder.

WHAT PSYCHIATRIC DRUGS CANNOT DO

When deciding whether or not to take a psychiatric drug, it is important for a patient to understand what such medications can and cannot do for them. In *The New Psychiatry*, Dr. Jack M. Gorman stresses how important it is that a patient be aware of whether or not their prescribed medication is working. "The one advantage of medication over other forms of psychiatric treatment is that an effect is usually discernible in a matter of weeks; no one should ever continue to take medication unless it is clear there is a benefit," he says. The effect of psychiatric drugs—usually quite concrete—is to relieve and sometimes eliminate specific symptoms. In order to not expect more from a drug than it can do, he encourages patients to realize that psychiatric drugs cannot improve one's basic personality; give one job success or a better marriage; make one smarter, more athletic, or a better parent.

Psychiatric drugs can, however, relieve symptoms that may be hindering an individual's performance in these areas. As a result, successful treatment often leads to more happiness and success at work and school and in relationships—so in this sense, psychiatric drugs do enable many individuals to find a better quality of life.

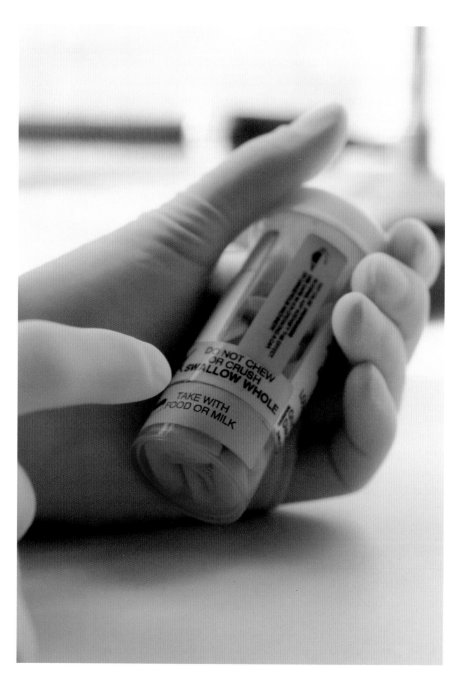

It is important to follow medication instructions exactly.

6 | Case Studies

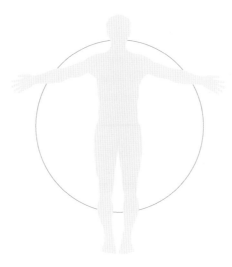

While each individual who experiences a personality disorder is unique, many have some things in common. For some, drug therapy will help them handle their symptoms; others will need to seek out other treatment.

BORDERLINE PERSONALITY DISORDER

When Sheila first went to see Dr. Raynor, she was twenty-seven years old, on the verge of a divorce from her second husband, and still trying to "decide what I want to be when I grow up and figure out who I am," as she told the psychiatrist with a humorless laugh.

In her sessions with Dr. Raynor over the next few months, Sheila gave some of the details of her life. Although she had graduated with a degree in elementary education, Sheila taught second grade for only six months before she decided she "just wasn't cut out to be a teacher." She spent the next year trying to freelance as a writer but discovered she couldn't stand the solitude of working alone each day. She started off every morning full of ideas for her writing, but by mid-morning, the emptiness of her apartment seemed to echo the enormous void Sheila felt inside herself. By lunchtime, she was frantic to avoid being alone anymore, in part because she couldn't push away the recurring thoughts that she was alone because no one wanted to be with her.

"That's not really true, I know. I mean, I chose a job that meant I had to be alone a lot," she told Dr. Raynor. "But I couldn't help *feeling* like it was true, you know? If people knew what I was really like inside . . ." Sheila broke off, then changed the subject. "My real problem right now is trying to keep this marriage together."

The therapist asked Sheila to give him more information about her first marriage and the time she had spent alone after it failed. She explained how, during those lonely months she'd begun working as a freelance writer, she had started spending each evening at a neighborhood pub. Though she had almost no close personal friends, at the pub she could talk for several hours each night and feel as though she was connecting with other people. One night, she met a man named Rick at the bar, and she impulsively married him within a week.

"That was certainly not one of my better decisions," Sheila said bitterly. "Rick turned out to be a real loser. He even beat me up a couple of times, right before he disappeared with most of my savings account and the only real gold jewelry I owned. We didn't even get a divorce—he just had the marriage annulled."

Sheila went on to admit that even though she knew that Rick had had serious problems of his own, something deep inside made her worry that his real reason for leaving her was that he'd found out how evil she was. "Most people don't understand," she told the doctor. "They'd never want anything to do with me if they knew."

After her failed attempt at freelance writing and her annulled marriage, Sheila returned to the university to pursue a graduate degree in counseling. However, she left the university just two weeks before she graduated in order to take a position in New York City as an apprentice jewelry designer, another position that turned out to be short lived.

"I thought I would love designing jewelry," she said. "I was so sure of it that I didn't even hesitate to give up on the counseling degree. It seemed like a dream come true—to get a chance to do something so artistic! But within just a few months, I felt like the people I was working with were starting to see through me. I think if I had stayed there, they might have had trouble because of me. I knew I had to leave." Sheila's face grew sad for a moment, and then she smiled. "But one good thing happened while I was there—I met Dan, my husband."

Dan Sutherlin, ten years Sheila's senior, was a buyer for a large chain of department stores. He met Sheila on one of his buying trips to New York City, and they married six months later. Almost immediately, however, problems began. Still unsure of her own career path, Sheila resented Dan's success and his confident enjoyment of his job.

"Everything just seems to fall into place for Dan," she complained. "Here I am, knocking myself out to find a job that fits me, with no clue where I'm going. I mean, I slaved away until I almost got a master's degree, and I have nothing to show for it! On the other hand, Dan started out stocking shelves in a department store to work his way through college, and instead, he worked his way up the ladder. He never even finished his bachelor's degree, and look at him now—he makes plenty of money, he loves what he's doing, he gets to travel, and everybody thinks he's just great. Why can't I find a job like that? I've worked much harder than he has!"

Sheila flip-flopped back and forth between loving Dan and being intensely angry at him for succeeding the way he had. One day she'd seem to be a loving wife, appreciative of his support and affection. The next, her resentment at his success would take over. She began to strike out at Dan by scheming to ruin him financially.

Dan, always generous with his money and willing to share everything with his new wife, was shocked when he discovered at the end of the month that Sheila had run up many thousands of dollars on their joint credit cards. In the argument that followed, Dan became furious and even questioned his choice of Sheila as a wife. Devastated, Sheila begged for forgiveness, promising dramatically never to spend another unnecessary dime. Dan was still too angry to make up, however; he slammed the door loudly behind him as he stormed outside and drove away.

Certain she was losing Dan, Sheila cut her wrists that night—not enough to end her life, but enough to frighten Dan badly when he arrived home some time later and found her bleeding profusely onto their expensive paisley bed-spread. After that, Dan kept a much more careful eye on their credit card accounts, behavior that Sheila interpreted one moment as Dan's being unbearably controlling and the next moment as proof that he now knew how evil she really was and was getting ready to abandon her.

As Sheila and Dan argued more and more, he began threatening to divorce her. Many times over the course of the next year, Sheila cut at her arms and legs until they bled, then healed and scarred over. Somehow, the pain and the blood diverted her thoughts for a brief time from the one thing that terrified her most—that Dan would leave her.

Meanwhile, she was searching desperately for a career that would give her life meaning and stability, but she

Someone who has a personality disorder may become suicidal if their condition is not treated.

seemed unable to hold down a job for more than a few weeks. Sheila's moods grew more and more unpredictable, and her behavior was full of angry outbursts, alienating even the few family members she had once considered friends and confidants, a situation that only confirmed her suspicions—that when people really got to know her and how evil she was, they didn't want anything to do with her.

When Dr. Raynor tried to point out to Sheila that some of her many problems might be due to her behavior, Sheila didn't seem to understand what he meant. "What are you

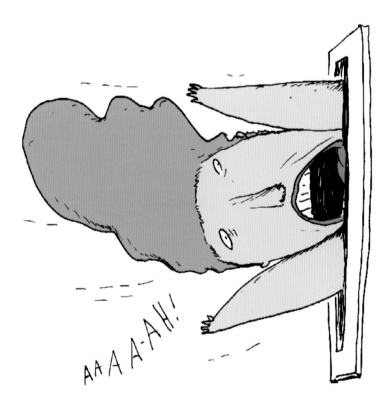

A person with a personality disorder may be unable to cope with high levels of anxiety!

talking about?" she demanded. "This is who I *am*. I can't change who I am!"

One afternoon, near the end of one of their sessions, Dr. Raynor reminded Sheila of information she had known for some time—that they would not be having an appointment the following week, since he would be away on vacation. Sheila immediately lost her temper even more violently than usual and began shouting at the doctor that he was "abandoning" her. It took several minutes before she could control her anger, but when the doctor was able to make her realize that their appointments would continue as usual after his vacation, she was overcome by guilt and shame at her display of temper. Now she was convinced once again that she was a truly evil person inside.

As Sheila's therapy continued, Dr. Raynor learned more about her background. Her parents had had a stormy relationship marked by frequent separations. Sheila often arrived home from school to find that one or the other of her parents had stormed out of the house in anger, and that parent would sometimes remain gone for as long as two or three months. At one point, both parents disappeared for more than six months, during which time Sheila stayed with an aunt and uncle. The uncle sexually molested her during those months, but when Sheila finally found the courage to tell her aunt, she not only received no help, she was accused of lying.

Sheila's anxiety about the impending breakup of her marriage to Dan and her inability to find a satisfying career left her depressed and nearly unable to function. Dr. Raynor prescribed a TCA for her, but the medication made Sheila's hostility and impulsivity even worse. While she was on it, she cut her arms and legs more frequently than she had before. The doctor then switched her to one of the SSRIs, fluoxetine (Prozac), which eventually relieved some of her

Psychopharmacotherapy

The following principles are valuable for those involved in drug treatment of mental disorders:

1. A thorough diagnostic assessment is the foundation of treatment.
2. Medications alone do not usually enable a person to recover completely.
3. Duration of treatment is very important; some patients require only short-term care, but others may need treatment for a lifetime.
4. History of an individual patient's (or that of the patient's family's) good or bad response to a specific treatment can provide guidance to further treatment.
5. It is important to watch carefully for any side effects that may develop throughout the duration of the treatment, using laboratory tests to monitor the patient.

Adapted from *Psychopathology & Function, Second Edition,* by Bette R. Bonder.

---

depression and irritability. At the same time, combined behavioral and cognitive therapies began providing some help. Sheila's therapy continued for several years, as is common in cases of borderline personality disorder.

PARANOID PERSONALITY DISORDER

Trent Cooper was always worried that someone was out to get him. If it wasn't his boss, it was a co-worker; if it wasn't a co-worker, it was his wife. He frequently summed up his feelings about the trustworthiness of his fellow humans by saying, "A person can never be too careful."

When Trent was in college, he became convinced that his roommate was plotting with some friends to hurt him. His only "evidence" was that at times, when Trent entered his dorm room, his roommate and friends would suddenly break off their conversation, and then greet him. This convinced Trent they had been talking about him while he was out of the room. Their greetings seemed forced and insincere to Trent, which only convinced him further that they were "up to something."

Although Trent's roommate tried to keep in touch with him after they graduated, Trent refused to respond to his calls or e-mails, certain that the roommate had done him a great wrong he could never forgive.

Trent eventually took a job in the post office, but his relationship with his boss and fellow workers was stormy. Other employees at the post office soon learned that getting to know Trent was impossible. To even the friendliest query about his family or college years, Trent simply responded that it was nobody's business. The other employees could not have imagined how many hours of anxiety their questions caused Trent. He mulled over even their most innocent questions for hours during his evenings alone, sure that any information he might have inadvertently given away would be used against him.

When his boss complimented him on a job well done, Trent heard only an attempt to make him work harder. One day during the holiday period when mail volume was unusually heavy, a more experienced worker offered to help Trent. Trent, however, responded angrily, convinced that the other worker's offer was actually a veiled criticism—implying that Trent was working much too slowly.

Angela was just the opposite of Trent. She had an open, friendly manner, and her warmth attracted many friends—both male and female. Most of them were puzzled by what she could possibly see in Trent, but she interpreted his aloofness and quietness as a kind of strength, and she married him after their first year of going out together. During that year, there had been signs that Trent was jealous of her

Medication as part of psychiatric treatment can help control psychotic episodes.

friendships with other men, but Angela felt his actions were a kind of compliment to her. The way she saw it, he loved her so much that he simply wanted to be sure she was totally his.

After they married, however, his jealousy began to look much different to her. Day after day he provoked arguments with his suspicions that she was having an affair. Angela had to account for every minute of her day, every verbal interchange with other people described in detail. Trent, however, had little or nothing to describe, since by this time he had only the most superficial of relationships with the people at work.

At the same time, Trent seemed to grow even more distant, causing Angela to doubt that he loved her at all. He seemed to be always on guard, watching her for the slightest hint that she was hiding something from him. She could tell from the way things were rearranged that he was going through her dresser drawers from time to time, and she suspected that he was searching for clues about her imagined unfaithfulness. When Angela caught him following her around on her lunch hour, however, she reached a breaking point and threatened to leave him if he did not go for counseling.

Trent met with a therapist a few times, but he said little except to complain about Angela's unfaithfulness. He also made a few sarcastic comments about psychiatrists who tried to find out personal information so they could "use it against people."

Trent and Angela's marriage limped along for another year at this uncomfortable level, until Trent's symptoms began to get more serious. When Angela gave him a computer for a birthday present, he began spending a great deal of time on-line. She learned eventually that he had become part of a small web ring with other people who believed they were being pursued or persecuted. Not long after this, Trent came under much greater pressure at work. A new supervisor was brought in who strongly emphasized teamwork. He pointed out many of Trent's failures to get along with his coworkers, angering Trent to the point of fury.

Trent then began experiencing brief psychotic episodes. At first, a voice told him what a terrible person he was and that he would soon die. The voice was so clear that Trent actually looked around to see who was speaking, and he insisted to Angela that he knew she could hear it, too. These hallucinations lasted only a short while, usually less than an hour, but Angela was terrified to see Trent so completely out of touch with reality.

One day Trent experienced a brief psychotic episode at work. His coworkers had no idea what to do, so they called

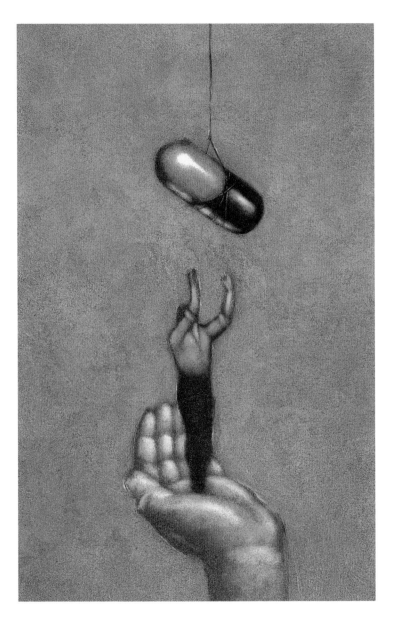

Drugs provide no simple answers to people with personality disorders, but medication does offer people help in dealing with their disease.

Angela. She in turn called his former therapist, who told her to get Trent to the hospital immediately. There, the psychiatrist did a complete evaluation and prescribed an antipsychotic drug called haloperidol (Haldol) to help Trent.

"Haldol will probably calm him down within a few hours," the psychiatrist told Angela, "but he needs to be on it for up to two weeks before you'll see any real change, and it may take months before he gets the full benefit of the drug. It's important that he get good follow-up care, too," he added, explaining that Haldol is one of the drugs that can cause tardive dyskinesia (involuntary muscle movements, particularly of the mouth and tongue) if used for too long a period of time. He also instructed Trent and Angela that it was very important for Trent to get back into his therapy program, adding that they should plan on his being in counseling for many months—perhaps even for years.

After six months on the haloperidol, Trent's psychotic episodes had diminished greatly. He was frightened enough by these episodes, and by Angela's renewed threats to leave him, to get back into therapy. Angela helped him find a new therapist, one with whom he felt safer, and he was able to open up a little more. Trent's therapy continues today.

SUMMARY

There are no easy answers for the people who experience personality disorders. But drug treatment can help them handle the symptoms of their disorders, allowing them to live more satisfying and productive lives. They will also need ongoing supplemental therapy (counseling and behavioral therapy, for instance). These various treatment programs give hope to the individuals who face these disorders.

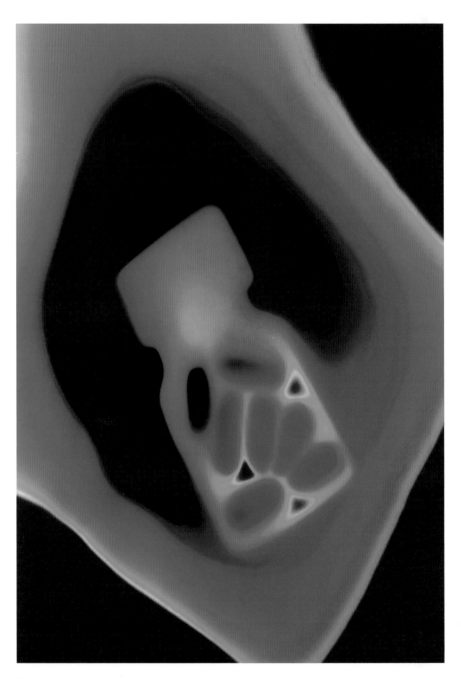

Psychiatric drugs are powerful chemicals that should be taken only under the supervision of a qualified medical practitioner.

7 | Risks and Side Effects

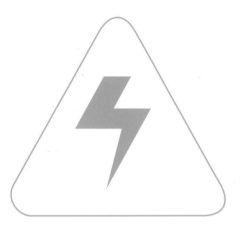

All drugs have the potential to interact with other drugs, sometimes causing dangerous and even deadly reactions, so all medications should be taken under the care and supervision of a qualified medical doctor, psychiatrist, or advanced practice nurse.

ANTIPSYCHOTICS

Haloperidol (Haldol) can cause neuroleptic malignant syndrome, as can all the antipsychotics. This syndrome is rare but causes fever, muscle rigidity, changes in mental status, and changes in pulse and blood pressure; it has the potential to be fatal. These drugs also have the potential to cause tardive dyskinesia, a disorder of involuntary muscle movements, particularly of the mouth and tongue.

Among other negative effects, severe sunburns may occur in people who are taking haloperidol. This drug should not be used with alcohol, as the combination of the two can significantly lower blood pressure.

Extra caution must be exercised in using Haldol if the patient is taking other drugs, as haloperidol can interact negatively with drugs in several other classes.

Haldol's side effects include sedation, dry mouth, constipation, blurry vision, low blood pressure, fatigue, *ataraxia*, weight gain, menstrual irregularities, *akathisia*, sexual dysfunction, *pseudoparkinsonism*, and tardive dyskinesia.

MOOD STABILIZERS

Carbamazepine (Tegretol) has many possible risks and side effects, including two blood disorders that can be fatal: aplastic anemia and agranulocytosis. Although these two disorders are unlikely to occur, patients must be closely monitored while they are taking this drug. Carbamazepine can also worsen the symptoms of *glaucoma*.

Carbamazepine should not be used during pregnancy as it can cause *spina bifida* and other problems in babies. It should not be taken in combination with MAOIs and should be taken with great caution if used with other drugs that cause sedation or central nervous system depression. Carbamazepine can negatively affect the reliability of contraceptives. It may also cause unusual bleeding, bruising, sores in the mouth, sore throat, or fever.

Valproate (Depakote) can cause liver failure and thrombocytopenia (a condition involving low blood platelets), and it too can make glaucoma symptoms worse. Valproate can cause spina bifida and other problems in babies. This drug should be taken with great caution if used with other drugs

GLOSSARY

ataraxia: A zombie-like feeling.

akathisia: Restlessness.

pseudoparkinsonism: Muscular tremor and rigidity.

glaucoma: An eye disorder in which increased pressure in the eye impairs vision and may eventually lead to blindness.

spina bifida: A defect in the spinal cord.

Pregnancy and Psychiatric Drugs

The effects of many psychiatric medicines during pregnancy have not been adequately researched. Some medications are known to cause birth defects, but for other drugs, there is not enough data to say for sure whether they are safe to take during pregnancy or not. Chemicals ingested by the mother will go to her unborn baby, so medication during pregnancy should only be used under a medical practitioner's supervision. In some cases, a woman's psychiatric condition may be so severe that she needs to stay on her medication; the risk to her own life (and her child's) would be greater without the drug than with it. Women who are taking psychotropic medication should always consult with their medical practitioner before becoming pregnant.

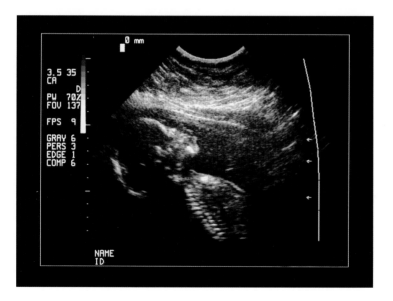

Psychiatric drugs can affect the development of an unborn child.

TCAs can affect heart function.

that cause sedation or central nervous system depression. Side effects of valproate may include some sedation, nausea, unsteady gait, and impaired muscle coordination, all of which may go away in the first week of use. Some loss of hair may occur in the first few months of use, but this symptom usually goes away. Valproate may also cause abdominal pain, yellow skin or eyes, liver impairment, and unusual bleeding or bruising.

Lithium can cause a condition known as lithium toxicity if the level of this drug becomes too high. Symptoms of lithium toxicity include: tremor, nausea, vomiting, mental confusion, slurred speech, lack of coordination, flu-like symptoms, and muscular weakness. If the patient experiences any of these symptoms, he should call his prescribing clinician immediately.

ANTIDEPRESSANTS

Tricyclic Antidepressants

TCAs such as imipramine (Tofranil), desipramine (Norpramin), and doxepin (Sinequan) can negatively affect heart function, and should not be taken by patients who have heart block, which is an abnormal heart rhythm, or by those who have recently had a heart attack.

TCAs should be used with extra caution by patients who have other psychiatric conditions, such as bipolar disorder, and physical conditions such as glaucoma, low blood pressure, or hyperthyroidism. These drugs can interact negatively with drugs of other classes, such as MAOIs.

Side effects may include blurry vision, constipation, dry mouth, fatigue, increased heart rate, low blood pressure, agitation, sweating, weight gain, insomnia, sexual dysfunction, and urinary difficulty.

Serotonin Syndrome

When there is more serotonin than needed in parts of the brain, patients may experience confusion, slurred speech, diaphoresis (excessive sweating), nausea, diarrhea, abdominal cramps, hyperreflexia (increased action of the reflexes), insomnia, problems with coagulation, and flushing. Excessive serotonin can be a result of taking more than one psychiatric drug at a time, or combining them in the wrong way. Serotonin syndrome can lead to seizures or death.

Selective Serotonin Reuptake Inhibitors

SSRIs include drugs such as fluoxetine (Prozac), sertraline (Zoloft), and paroxetine (Paxil). These drugs should not be taken with other SSRIs, because this may cause serotonin syndrome (see sidebar). Besides not combining SSRIs, they should not be taken with Saint-John's-wort, tryptophan, or MAOI antidepressants. These drugs may negatively affect patients with bipolar disorder, diabetes, epilepsy, or a psychotic disorder.

Side effects may include fatigue, nausea, weakness, sweating, decreased appetite, rash, sexual dysfunction, agitation, insomnia, anxiety, or tremor. All antidepressants need to be used cautiously when treating mood disorders, since they may trigger mania.

ANTIANXIETY DRUGS

Chlordiazepoxide (Librium) and diazepam (Valium) belong to a group of drugs known as the benzodiazepines. These drugs are physically and psychologically habit forming, so they must be used only under the care of a knowledgeable physician. Use of these drugs for longer than four weeks is not recommended. Seizures may occur if these drugs are stopped abruptly, so a physician should always be consulted when a patient wants to stop taking these drugs.

The benzodiazepines must not be used with alcohol, as the combination can cause an individual to stop breathing. These drugs should not be used during pregnancy because of the risk of birth defects. Elderly people are particularly sensitive to these drugs and may experience stronger side effects than a younger person may, even when taking low doses. Side effects may include sedation, memory impairment, poor muscle coordination, agitation, and insomnia. The benzodiazepines are usually only used for anxiety while

---

Off-Label Prescriptions

The FDA bases its approval on specific research results. Sometimes, a particular use for a drug may have been thoroughly researched by many studies, while other uses lack the same amount of research. In that case, the drug label will only include the uses that have met the FDA's stringent research requirements. Physicians, however, may continue to prescribe that drug for other "off-label" uses.

A medical practitioner can help individuals evaluate the pros and cons of taking medication.

the patient is getting started on an SSRI (since SSRIs take four to six weeks before they become effective).

SUMMARY

In *The New Psychiatry*, Jack Gorman, M.D., gives a simple summary of what a drug side effect is: "A side effect is anything a drug does that we don't want it to do," and explains that any chemical substance we put into out bodies will affect more than just the one part of our body that we want it to affect. He likens this to the food we eat, using a steak as an example of good taste and a good source of needed protein for our bodies. He then points out that steak can do other things to our bodies, however, including increase our cholesterol level and add unwanted weight. Some people will consider both these positive and negative effects of eating steak and decide to go ahead and eat the steak, because for them the benefits outweigh the risks. In much the same way, drugs can provide needed benefits, but also produce unwanted side effects, though some may be much more serious than the "side effects" of eating steak. And in some cases, the benefits will outweigh the side effects to the degree that many people suffering from anxiety disorders will decide they will take the drugs and find ways to deal with the side effects.

Eating a healthy diet and taking vitamins can help control the symptoms of personality disorders.

8 | Alternative and Supplementary Treatments

Many experts recommend alternative treatments for mental disorders. These are commonsense treatments that can be used both on their own and in combination with psychotherapy and pharmacotherapy.

DIET

A well-balanced diet that includes a variety of foods from each food group is one of the best ways to make sure our bodies are furnished with vital minerals and vitamins. When people don't get adequate nutrition, their bodies lack the necessary ingredients to perform properly, and illness is often the result. There are many examples of illnesses caused by vitamin and mineral deficiencies.

For instance, scurvy, a disease that causes bleeding from the mucous membranes, weakness, joint pain, and many other unpleasant symptoms, was a terrible problem to British sailors in past centuries. They would spend long months at sea, with limited foods to eat. Eventually it was discovered that their disease was caused by the lack of vitamin C. When they added limes to their diet, the scurvy disappeared. Other diseases, such as blindness, rickets, anemia, and even dementia, can in some cases be traced directly to vitamin deficiencies.

Eating enough calories each day is also important, as is spreading meals throughout the day so that blood sugar levels remain as stable as possible. According to author Edward Drummond, M.D., "Symptoms of many psychiatric disorders can intensify somewhat if you eat only one meal a day, or if you are not eating enough. For example, palpitations, tremor, sweating, restlessness, and irritability from anxiety can be more troublesome if you eat only a single meal."

Alcohol, caffeine, tobacco, and recreational drugs can worsen many common symptoms of mental disorders, particularly depression and anxiety. Even though alcohol can seem to help at first, by initially making an individual feel more relaxed, it can actually cause more problems later on.

EXERCISE

GLOSSARY

endorphins: *Naturally occurring proteins in the brain that act to raise the threshold of pain.*

Exercise helps people feel they are participating in the world and also "promotes feelings of strength, competence, and self-esteem," according to Drummond. Exercise can raise daytime energy levels and promote restful sleep at night. The feeling of being disciplined enough to continue any kind of regular exercise can help counteract negative feelings that come with many of the personality disorders. What's more, exercise can actually create a feeling of well-being by encouraging the body to produce ***endorphins***.

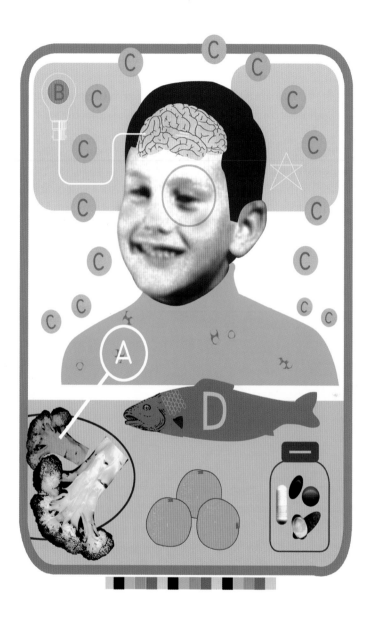

Vitamins play an important role in many body functions, including brain activity.

EDUCATION

The more a patient learns about her disease, the more understanding she will have of her symptoms and how to deal with them. Learning in this way helps give the patient more feeling of control and helps her make decisions about treatment.

Often, learning about mental disorders such as the personality disorders involves interaction with other people who either have the same disorder or who know someone else who does. Sharing experiences, symptoms, and treatments can alleviate the feeling of aloneness that pervades the lives of many people with personality disorders.

Regular exercise can help decrease psychiatric symptoms.

SELF-HELP GROUPS

Self-help groups help people who are suffering many different types of problems. When individuals suffering from the same or similar disorder meet regularly to share both their struggles and their progress, they provide important emotional support for one another. Those involved can also gain information and insight about their disorder.

CRISIS PLAN

Dealing with a health crisis, whether physical or mental, can be a difficult and confusing task. Even after a person's problem is diagnosed and appropriate therapies (either psychotherapy or pharmacotherapy) have been prescribed, the individual must still learn how to live a meaningful life within the context of her disease or disorder.

In her book *Winning Against Relapse*, Mary Ellen Copeland writes of her own struggle with manic depression, major depression, fibromyalgia, and chronic myofascial pain syndrome, and of her personal search for wellness and improvement in life quality. She was determined to get her "life back, to work and to play, to enjoy my family and friends."

To this end, Copeland and others created the Wellness Recovery Action Plan (WRAP), a "structured system for monitoring uncomfortable or distressing symptoms, as well as unhealthy habits or behavior patterns. Through planned responses, WRAP is also helpful in reducing, modifying, or eliminating those symptoms and/or creating the life change you want." Overall, the WRAP system not only helps people develop and maintain wellness skills and strategies, it also helps individuals to develop advanced directives.

Many people have found that Eastern relaxation techniques are effective tools for coping with anxiety and depression.

Copeland writes:

> Previous to the development of this plan, I thought that I was doing a really good job of managing my life while "putting up" with time when the depression and pain seemed overwhelming. Now, because of my WRAP, I have fewer episodes of depression and pain. I also notice when these episodes are starting and I can use my WRAP to "nip them in the bud," before they get out of control and are much more difficult to manage.

Many people have discovered that when they respond in such a way as to reduce, relieve, or eliminate their symptoms as they first appear, rather than waiting until those

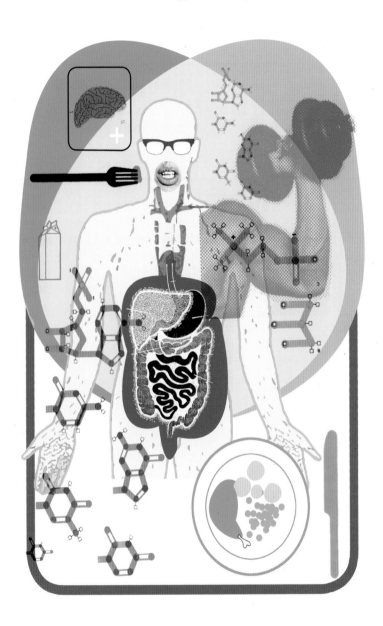

Exercise and a healthy diet promote mental and physical health.

The World Health Organization's definition of good health.

symptoms have become severe, they can significantly improve their level of wellness and their overall quality of life.

Copeland considers her WRAP a revisable wellness strategy, always adding new wellness strategies and alternative treatments as she finds them, thus developing her own combination of techniques that allow her to respond promptly and efficiently to her triggers and early warning signs.

WRAP includes five parts, as follows:

1. *Daily maintenance.* This includes the things an individual knows she must do every day in order to feel good. Daily maintenance means sensible eating, exercise, relaxation techniques, work, recreational activities, and contact with friends. It can also include extra activities, such as time with pets, making plans for vacations and other activities, laundry and housework, and appointments with mental health professionals.
2. *List of "triggers."* Triggers are external events or circumstances that may cause symptoms to begin. In some cases, early response to symptoms can keep them from worsening. Triggers may include: anniversary dates of a loss or a trauma; physical illness; criticism; conflict with family, friends, or co-workers; lack of sleep; and stress. Individuals who develop a WRAP create a plan to follow when they experience a trigger event or situation.
3. *List of early warning signs.* Early warning signs indicate to the individual that more action is necessary to prevent her symptoms from worsening. These signs may include such things as irritability, heightened anxiety, lack of motivation, and craving alcohol or drugs. Some people find that they are isolating themselves, not keeping appointments, or feeling unconnected to their body. In this instance, as in the

Information on People with Borderline Personality Disorder and Their Treatment

Jerome Kroll, in his book, *PTSD/Borderlines in Therapy*, lists the following eight points, not as proven fact, but as "evidence to be considered" in the treatment of patients with borderline personality disorder.

1. The effectiveness of psychotherapy with borderlines has not been demonstrated.
2. Fifty percent of borderlines quit therapy within six months.
3. Fifty percent of borderlines in successful therapy terminate therapy against the advice of their therapist.
4. Most borderlines improve around age thirty.
5. About eight to 15 percent of borderlines have committed suicide by the ten- to fifteen-year follow-up.
6. Suicide in borderlines is correlated with antisocial personality, ongoing alcohol abuse, and depression of an angry-hostile nature.
7. Suicide is negatively correlated with wrist cutting.
8. About 70 to 80 percent of borderlines appear to have experienced some form of sexual and/or physical abuse in childhood.

case of triggers, individuals create a plan for responding appropriately to early warning signs.

4. *Description of symptoms*. This list includes a description of what happens when an individual's situation is breaking down. The WRAP includes a plan for times when the patient realizes she is responding irrationally to events around her, withdrawing from her customary activities, sleeping excessively, thinking about doing harm to herself, and acting in risky ways.

5. *Advance directives*. In some cases, a patient's condition deteriorates to the point where he is no longer

able to make decisions for himself. When that happens, it is vital that he has a description of symptoms, medication, and people who can help. It is also important to have a plan that provides guidance as to his wishes regarding treatment facilities, treatments that help and those that should be avoided, and who can make decisions for him.

SUMMARY

For some individuals with personality disorders, their condition can last a lifetime. Using reasonable alternative treatments such as those listed in this chapter will not cure a patient's personality disorder any more than taking a particular drug will make the disorder magically disappear, but a combination of drug therapy and alternative treatments can go a long way toward creating a more ordered and rewarding lifestyle. In the end, these changes may help the patient to feel better about himself, a positive step that may also have some impact on his well-being.

FURTHER READING

Bonder, Bette R. *Psychopathology & Function, Second Edition.* Thorofare, N.J.: Slack, 1995.

Copeland, Mary Ellen. *Winning Against Relapse.* New York: New Harbinger Publications, 1998.

Drummond, Edward. *The Complete Guide to Psychiatric Drugs.* New York: John Wiley & Sons, 2000.

Gorman, Jack M. *The Essential Guide to Psychiatric Drugs.* New York: St. Martin's Griffin, 1997.

Gorman, Jack M. *The New Psychiatry.* New York: St. Martin's, 1996.

Kernberg, Otto F. *Severe Personality Disorders, Psychotherapeutic Strategies.* New Haven: Yale University Press, 1984.

Kroll, Jerome. *The Challenge of the Borderline Patient.* New York: W. W. Norton, 1988.

Kroll, Jerome. *PTSD/Borderlines in Therapy: Finding the Balance.* New York: W. W. Norton, 1993.

FOR MORE INFORMATION

American Psychiatric Association
1400 K St., N.W.
Washington, DC 20005
www.psych.org

American Psychological Association
750 First Street, N.E.
Washington, DC 20002
www.apa.org

Mental Help Net, on personality disorders
mentalhelp.net/poc/center_index.php?id=8

National Alliance for the Mentally Ill
200 North Glebe Road
Suite 1015
Arlington, VA 22203
800-950-NAMI

National Institute of Mental Health
Public Inquiries
5600 Fishers Lane
Room 7C-02
Rockville, MD 20857

National Mental Health Association
1021 Prince Street
Alexandria, VA 22314-2971

800-969-NMHA
www.nmha.org

On-line screening for personality disorders from New York
    University School of Medicine
www.med.nyu.edu/Psych/screens/pds.html

Personality Disorders Foundation
http://pdf.uchc.edu/

For an overview of the personality disorders, with links to
    other helpful web pages
www.personalityresearch.org/pd.html

Publisher's Note:

The Web sites listed on this page were active at the time of
publication. The publisher is not responsible for Web sites
that have changed their address or discontinued operation
since the date of publication. The publisher will review and
update the Web sites upon each reprint.

INDEX

BIOGRAPHIES

Shirley Brinkerhoff is a writer, editor, speaker, and musician. She graduated Summa Cum Laude from Cornerstone University with a Bachelor of Music degree, and from Western Michigan University with a Master of Music degree. She has published six young adult novels, ten informational books for young people, scores of short stories and articles, and teaches at writers' conferences throughout the United States.

Mary Ann Johnson is a licensed child and adolescent clinical nurse specialist and a family psychiatric nurse practitioner in the state of Massachusetts. She completed her psychotherapy training at Cambridge Hospital and her psychopharmacology training at Massachusetts General Hospital. She is the director of clinical trials in the pediatric psychopharmacology research unit at Massachusetts General Hospital.

Donald Esherick has spent seventeen years working in the pharmaceutical industry and is currently an associate director of Worldwide Regulatory Affairs with Wyeth Research in Philadelphia, Pennsylvania. He specializes in the chemistry section (manufacture and testing) of investigational and marketed drugs.